Alaska
Ports of Call

Portions of this book appear in *Fodor's Alaska*

Fodor's Travel Publications, Inc.
New York • Toronto • London • Sydney • Auckland
www.fodors.com

Fodor's Alaska Ports of Call

EDITOR: Deborah Kaufman

Editorial Contributors: Sue Kernaghan, Don Pitcher, Tom Reale, M. T. Schwartzman

Editorial Production: Linda K. Schmidt

Maps: David Lindroth, *cartographer*; Robert Blake, *map editor*

Design: Fabrizio La Rocca, *creative director*; Guido Caroti, *associate art director*; Jolie Novak, *photo editor*

Production/Manufacturing: Robert B. Shields

Cover Photo (Inupiat birch basket detail, Northwest Alaska): Pat O'Hara/ Tony Stone

Cover Design: Allison Saltzman

Copyright

ISBN 0–679–00366–5

ISSN 1520–0205

Special Sales

Fodor's Travel Publications are available at special discounts for bulk purchases for sales promotions or premiums. Special editions, including personalized covers, excerpts of existing guides, and corporate imprints, can be created in large quantities for special needs. For more information, contact your local bookseller or write to Special Markets, Fodor's Travel Publications, 201 East 50th Street, New York, NY 10022. Inquiries from Canada should be directed to your local Canadian bookseller or sent to Random House of Canada, Ltd., Marketing Department, 2775 Matheson Boulevard East, Mississauga, Ontario L4W 4P7. Inquiries from the United Kingdom should be sent to Fodor's Travel Publications, 20 Vauxhall Bridge Road, London SW1V 2SA, England.

PRINTED IN THE UNITED STATES OF AMERICA

10 9 8 7 6 5 4 3 2 1

CONTENTS

4   The Alaska Cruise Fleet   108

Index   122

Maps

Don't Forget to Write

Keeping a travel guide fresh and up-to-date is a big job. So we love your feedback—positive and negative—and follow up on all suggestions. Contact the *Alaska Ports of Call* editor at editors@fodors.com or c/o Fodor's, 201 East 50th Street, New York, New York 10022. And have a wonderful trip!

Important Tip

Although all prices, opening times, and other details in this book are based on information supplied to us at press time, changes occur all the time in the travel world, and Fodor's cannot accept responsibility for facts that become outdated or for inadvertent errors or omissions. So **always confirm information when it matters,** especially if you're making a detour to visit a specific place.

Karen Cure
Editorial Director

THE CHARACTER OF ALASKA

When I took my first cruise to Alaska, I was drawn by the imagery, bigger than life, associated with the 49th American state. After all, it's called "The Great Land," a loose translation of the Aleut word "Alyeska." Alaska boasts the highest mountain in North America—Denali, "The High One" in the Athabascan tongue—as well as 17 of the 20 highest peaks in the United States. There are more bald eagles here than anywhere else, more totem poles, thousands of glaciers, and king-size salmon and humongous halibut.

There is nothing ordinary about this land—or the people who call it home. The "Last Frontier" demands self-sufficiency, ingenuity, and bravery, and the people of Alaska embody a spirit of adventure and independence. Status in Alaska is measured by longevity. Newcomers are called cheechakos. Old-timers are known as sourdoughs. But the greatest honor is reserved for the pioneers, those who have spent the most time in the country—at least 30 years.

I have a great affinity for Alaska and its people, even though I live far across the continent, outside New York City, where our mountains are skyscrapers and wildlife means mostly pigeons. My home is not much of a frontier, but deep inside me—as in, I suspect, so many Americans—there is a need for space. Room to roam is something Alaska has in abundance. Alaska is the largest state in the Union; its 586,412 square miles equal one-fifth the land mass of the Lower 48. A popular postcard shows Alaska superimposed on a map of the United States: It stretches nearly from sea to shining sea. (Look for this postcard in souvenir shops.)

Today's Alaskan combines tenacity and technology to live in a land that remains challenging. Like the towering mountains and deep fjords that line the Inside Passage, the Alaskan character has been shaped by the elements. All of southeast Alaska lies in a rain forest (Ketchikan receives more than 150 inches of rain a year), and except for Haines and Skagway in the north, there are no roads linking the towns along the Panhandle. In fact, Juneau is the only state capital in the United States that cannot be reached over land. You fly in or you sail in, but you don't drive in.

Geography alone makes Alaska an ideal cruise destination. On a typical seven-day itinerary you'll visit up to four ports of call and one or two scenic bays or fjords. And the nature of ship travel is perfectly suited to discovering what

Alaska is all about. From the deck of a cruise ship, you can come face to face with a glacier. From the dining room, you can watch a full moon rise over a snow-striped mountain. And you can enjoy it all in the lap of luxury.

The natural beauty of Alaska is hard to overstate. As you prepare for your cruise, consider these facts about Alaska's grandeur:

● The Inside Passage, the traditional route north to Alaska and a favorite among cruise passengers, stretches 1,000 miles from Puget Sound, Washington, in the south to Skagway, Alaska, in the north. From there, the Gulf of Alaska arcs for another 500 miles from east to west.

● Alaska has thousands of glaciers. No one really knows how many, but estimates range from 5,000 to 100,000. Among the most famous ones that cruise passengers visit are LeConte outside Petersburg, the southernmost calving glacier in North America, and Hubbard at Yakutat Bay in the Gulf of Alaska, 6 miles wide and 76 miles long to its source. There are 12 tidewater glaciers in Glacier Bay National Park and Preserve and another 16 glaciers in College Fjord off Prince William Sound. The Malaspina Glacier, at the entrance to Yakutat Bay, is bigger than the state of Rhode Island.

● Tongass National Forest, which spans great stretches of the Inside Passage, is the largest national forest in the United States. Wrangell-St. Elias National Park, a UNESCO World Heritage Site east of Anchorage and bordering the Gulf of Alaska, is the largest national park in the United States— six times the size of Yellowstone.

In such broad expanses of land, airplanes have become as common as taxis in New York. The bush plane in particular holds a special place in Alaskan folklore: this was the machine that opened the wilderness and that provides the only access to remote communities to this day. In South Anchorage, a suburb just beyond downtown, propeller planes are parked one after another like the family car. Lake Hood, near the airport, is the world's largest and busiest seaplane base; if you have time, be sure to stop by to watch the brightly painted Cessnas and De Havilland Beavers coming and going hourly. Anchorage pays special tribute to the bush pilots of the past. Two museums, the Alaska Aviation Heritage Museum and the Reeve Aviation Picture Museum, are dedicated to their exploits. Even today, the bush pilot is a revered figure, and I can think of few better ways to appreciate the character of the people and the wonder of the land than from the window of a Cessna.

Mere numbers cannot capture the effect of Alaska on the human spirit. Before I went to Alaska, I'd never seen anyone catch her breath. Yet this was the genuine reaction of my traveling companion as she saw her first glacier—the mighty Mendenhall, its icy face peeking out from a veil of mist just 13 miles from downtown Juneau. While driving back to the pier, we passed Salmon Creek, where the annual salmon run was in full swing. The water was so thick with fish we could have waded in and plucked one out.

Wildlife is everywhere in Alaska. The state has 15 species of whales. Southeast Alaska has more brown bears than the rest of the United States combined. And Alaska ranks number one in bald eagles (Florida is number two).

Bird-watchers will have a field day looking for bald eagles. These birds have long represented courage and power, so it is appropriate that so many of them populate Alaska. In fact, eagles are so numerous you'll have to remind yourself that they remain a threatened species. There's even an eagle hospital, the Alaska Raptor Rehabilitation Center in Sitka, where injured eagles and other birds of prey are nursed back to health. You can visit the center if your ship calls in Ketchikan. If not, bald eagles are easily spotted in the wild: look for their bright white heads perched high in the treetops—or atop telephone poles—all along the Inside Passage.

You may also run into whales during your cruise. On my second cruise to Alaska, our small ship happened upon a couple of sleeping whales, their blue-black bodies barely breaking the surface of the water. The captain cut the engines so we wouldn't disturb the whales' slumber, and for a good while we just observed their breathing. Later the whole scene was replayed in the main lounge on videotape.

Not long afterward we experienced another Kodak moment: a brown bear foraging on the shoreline. Again, the captain held our position as the bear wandered along the water's edge. When the bear was done, he moved on, as did we. The captain, however, had something more in store for us. At a rushing waterfall, he nudged the bow of our small ship under the gush of water. Raincoat-clad crew members filled pitchers with glacial runoff, and soon we all enjoyed a refreshment of cool mineral water. Such are the simple pleasures of an Alaskan cruise: calving glaciers, sea lions and seals, and sensational sunsets—at midnight.

In addition to glaciers and wildlife, there's an exciting frontier history to discover. You will be just the latest in a long line of visitors who have come here over the ages. Scientists estimate that the first people arrived in Alaska some 15,000 years ago, when they migrated across the Bering Land Bridge from Asia. (Some expedition ships sail from Alaska to the Russian Far East, allowing you to follow the migration pattern in reverse.) The earliest evidence of human habitation along the Inside Passage can be found in Wrangell, where petroglyphs—mysterious markings carved into rocks and boulders on the beach—are thought to be at least 8,000 years old.

Alaska's indigenous people belong to one of four groups: Aleuts, Athabascans, Eskimos, and Northwest Coast Indians. The Aleuts live on the Aleutian Islands. Athabascans populate the Interior, while Eskimos inhabit the Arctic regions of the Far North. The Native Alaskans you are most likely to meet during your cruise are the Tlingit, Haida, or Tsimshian people of the Inside Passage.

The Tlingit are responsible for Alaska's famous totem carvings. Totem poles tell the story of a great event, identify members of the same clan, and honor great leaders. The best place to see totem poles is Saxman Native Village in Ketchikan, where you'll find my favorite—the Abraham Lincoln totem pole, with an image of Honest Abe at its top. Don't miss the collection of original totems at the Totem Heritage Center. These are the oldest authentic poles in Alaska, some dating back about 200 years. Today, you can still see

Native artisans at work in Ketchikan, Haines, and Sitka, where the totem poles are lesser known but equally impressive.

Northwest Coast Indians are noted for their many artistic skills; totem carvings are just the most celebrated example. Miniature totem reproductions are among the most popular souvenirs in Alaska, but ceremonial masks, decorative paddles, and woven baskets also make great gifts. These and other Native crafts are sold throughout the Inside Passage. Before you buy, look for the Silver Hand label, which guarantees authenticity. (For non-Native items, check for the "Made in Alaska" polar bear logo.)

Buying local crafts is just one way for cruise passengers to appreciate the local culture. Native Alaskans are often happy to show you around. In Juneau, Ketchikan, and Sitka, you can book a sightseeing tour with a Native point of view. Performances of Native dance and traditional storytelling entertain visitors in Juneau, Sitka, and Haines. Ask about these aboard your ship or at the visitor information office near the pier.

In the footsteps of Native Alaskans came European explorers. The first was Vitus Bering, who "discovered" Alaska and claimed it for Russia in 1741. The Russians made Kodiak their capital before moving the seat of government to Sitka in 1808. Next came British and Spanish explorers. Cook Inlet in Anchorage is named for British explorer Captain Cook; a statue of him dominates Resolution Park, a terraced lookout perched above the inlet that bears his name. One member of Cook's expedition was George Vancouver, namesake of the Canadian port city where most Alaska cruises begin or end. Ketchikan sits on an island named after a Spaniard, the Count of Revillagigedo, viceroy of New Spain and a proponent of Spanish exploration of Alaska. Wrangell Island, at the southern end of the Inside Passage, is the only Alaskan port of call to have flown three flags—Russian, British, and finally American.

The connection with Europe is echoed in the nicknames given to some of Alaska's port cities. Valdez is often referred to as Alaska's "Little Switzerland" for the mountains that ring the city. Petersburg is Alaska's "Little Norway," and the town's residents still celebrate their Scandinavian heritage every May in a festival of Norwegian song and dance. If you are lucky enough to visit Petersburg on your cruise (only the smallest ships and ferries call here), you may be treated to a performance at the Sons of Norway Hall—followed by a Norwegian smorgasbord.

Russia sold Alaska to the United States in 1867 for $7.2 million, or about 2¢ an acre. Secretary of State William H. Seward, who orchestrated the purchase, was publicly ridiculed for his "folly." But opinions changed when word got out that gold had been discovered in the Far North; the news set off a stampede of legendary proportion. The Gold Rush, perhaps the most colorful episode in Alaska's storied history, reached a fever pitch during the winter of 1897-98. Some say up to 100,000 men headed for the gold fields. More conservative estimates put the number as low as 30,000. In either case, the Klondike Gold Rush put Alaska on the map, as gold-crazed prospectors, con men, and assorted other characters clamored up the Inside Passage.

The Gold Rush has held a life-long fascination for me. As a child, I first read Jack London's accounts of the heady Gold Rush days, and I still have my original color-illustrated copy of *Call of the Wild*. This classic novel, based on London's personal experiences, is required reading for anyone cruising Alaska. Also be sure to see the Walt Disney adaptation of London's *White Fang*; it was filmed on location in Haines.

If, like me, you're an aficionado of Gold Rush history, choose a cruise that includes a call at Skagway, the gateway to the Klondike of a century ago. As you sail the Lynn Canal, the natural channel that connects Skagway with the rest of the Inside Passage, keep in mind that you are following the same route and traveling in the same manner (albeit a bit more luxuriously) as the original prospectors. Once ashore, you'll hear the story of Frank Reid (the good guy) and Jefferson Randolph "Soapy" Smith (the bad guy), who shot it out for control of Skagway. You'll hear how superintendent Samuel Steele of the Canadian Mounted Police called Skagway "the roughest place on earth." And you'll learn how, after the Gold Rush died down, Skagway became the birthplace of Alaska's tourism industry.

Today, the town of Skagway looks much as it did in the early 1900s. The entire downtown area is a National Historic District, part of Klondike Gold Rush National Historic Park. The yellow 1930s touring limousines you see are operated by the Skagway Streetcar Company, which re-creates Martin Itjen's original Skagway sightseeing tour. This is a very popular shore excursion, as is a ride on the vintage parlor cars of the White Pass and Yukon Railway (see Chapter 3). It's one of the few chances cruise passengers have to venture deep into the mountains—just as prospectors traveled over the treacherous White Pass. From the cars of the train, you can still see the "Trail of '98," a footpath worn permanently into the mountainside.

Few establishments evoke the spirit of the frontier like the local saloon, and as a cruise passenger (depending on your itinerary) you'll have the opportunity to visit two of Alaska's most famous ones. Near the cruise ship docks in Skagway is the Red Onion Saloon— one of my favorite places in Alaska. To step inside is to return to 1898, when the saloon was founded; the bartender still serves drinks on the original mahogany bar. In Juneau, another Gold-Rush town, the Red Dog Saloon has been a favorite local watering hole since early this century. In fact, Wyatt Earp's six-shooter still hangs on the wall. It's said he left it here while just passing through.

Like Wyatt Earp, you too will just be passing through. But, as you are about to discover, cruising is a great way to see "The Great Land." I encourage you to spend as much time as you can in Alaska. Bring plenty of film or videotape, don't forget a rain slicker, and do try everything. Go hiking, fishing, flightseeing. Ride the railroads, book a salmon bake, scope for eagles. Think big—and be sure to buy a souvenir totem pole.

—M. T. Schwartzman

1 Cruise Primer

ALASKA, IT WOULD SEEM, was made for cruising. The traditional route to the state is by sea, through a 1,000-mi-long protected waterway known as the Inside Passage. From Vancouver in the south to Skagway in the north, it winds around islands large and small, past glacier-carved fjords and hemlock-blanketed mountains. This great land is home to breaching whales, nesting eagles, spawning salmon, and calving glaciers. The towns here can be reached only by air or sea. There are no roads; Juneau, in fact, is the only water-locked state capital in the United States. Beyond the Inside Passage, the Gulf of Alaska leads to Prince William Sound—famous for its marine life and more fjords and glaciers—and Anchorage, Alaska's largest city.

An Alaska cruise is no longer the exclusive privilege of retirees. Following the latest trend in cruising, more and more families are setting sail for Alaska. The peak season falls during summer school vacation, so kids are now a common sight aboard ship. Cruise lines have responded with programs designed specifically for children and with some discount shore excursions for kids under 12. Shore excursions have become more active, too, often incorporating activities families can enjoy together, such as bicycling, kayaking, and hiking.

For adults, too, the cruise lines now offer more than ever before. Alaska is one of cruising's showcase destinations, so the lines are putting their grandest ships up here.

Itineraries give passengers more choices than ever before— from Bering Strait cruises, which include a crossing to the Russian Far East, to the traditional loop cruises of the Inside Passage, round-trip from Vancouver. A few smaller boats sail only in Prince William Sound, away from big-ship traffic.

Bingo and bridge tournaments, deck games, contests, demonstrations, and lectures are offered daily. You'll also find trendier pursuits: computer classes, stress-management seminars, and talks on financial planning. Enrichment programs are becoming increasingly popular. Some lines hire celebrity or Native speakers, naturalists, or local personalities.

On the big ocean liners, you can eat practically all day and night. There's often a selection of healthy choices for nutrition-conscious eaters. Some ships coordinate your dining-room meals with your exercise program in the health club.

Luxury ships are not your only option for traveling to Alaska. There are small coastal ships and one rugged expedition-type vessel. And for more independent types, there's no better way to see Alaska than aboard the ferries of the Alaska Marine Highway System, which allow you to travel with your car or RV and explore at your own pace.

CHOOSING YOUR CRUISE

Every ship has its own personality, depending on its size, the year it was built, and its intended purpose. Big ships are more stable and offer a huge variety of activities and facilities. Smaller ships feel intimate, like private clubs. Each type of ship satisfies a certain type of passenger, and for every big-ship fan there is someone who would never set foot aboard one of these "floating resorts."

The type of ship you choose is the most important factor in your Alaska cruise vacation because it will determine how you see Alaska. Big ships sail farther from land and visit major ports of call such as Juneau, Skagway, and Ketchikan. Small ships spend much of their time hugging the coastline, looking for wildlife, waterfalls, and other natural and scenic attractions.

Types of Ships

Ocean Liners

Alaska's ocean-liner fleet represents the very best that today's cruise industry has to offer. Nearly all the ships were built within the last two decades and have atrium lobbies, state-of-the-art health spas, high-tech show lounges, and elaborate dining rooms. They are a comfortable and sometimes even luxurious way to tour Alaska's major ports of call and scenic attractions. By night they come alive with Vegas-style revues, pulsating discos, and somewhat more sedate cabaret or comedy acts. Some of the latest liners have cabins with verandas—a great bonus in Alaska for watching the scenery go by from the privacy of your own stateroom. The newest cruise ships are lined with glass throughout their corridors and public rooms, so you're never far from the sea—or a great view of "The Great Land."

Expedition Ships

Vessels of this type are designed to reach into the most remote corners of the world. Shallow drafts allow them to navigate up rivers, close to coastlines, and into shallow coves. Hulls may be hardened for sailing in Antarctic ice. Motorized rubber landing craft, known as Zodiacs, are kept on board, making it possible for passengers to put ashore almost anywhere. However, because the emphasis during cruises aboard expedition ships tends to be on learning and exploring, the ships don't have casinos, shows, multiple bars and lounges, and other typical diversions. Instead, for entertainment they have theaters for lectures, well-stocked libraries, and enrichment programs led by experts. At press time there was only one expedition ship, the *World Discoverer* (*see* Chapter 4), making trips to Alaska.

Coastal Cruisers

Designed more for exploring than entertaining, these are smaller than the expedition ships. They, too, are able to sail to remote waterways and ports, but unlike the expedition ships, they do not have ice-hardened hulls. Some have forward gangways for bow landings or carry a fleet of Zodiac landing craft. Coastal cruisers offer few on-board facilities and public spaces—perhaps just a dining room and a lounge.

Ferries

The state ferry system is known as the Alaska Marine Highway because its vessels carry vehicles as well as passengers. Each ferry has a car deck that can accommodate every size vehicle from the family car to a Winnebago. This capability presents an opportunity for independent travelers with wanderlust: you can take your vehicle ashore, drive around, even live in it, and then transport it with you to the next port of call. Once the ferry reaches Skagway or Haines (the only Inside Passage towns connected to a road system), you can drive farther north to Fairbanks and Anchorage by way of the Alaska Highway.

Itineraries

Alaska sailings come chiefly in two varieties: round-trip Inside Passage loops and one-way Inside Passage–Gulf of Alaska cruises. Both itineraries are typically seven days. However, if you want to combine a land tour with your Inside Passage loop, you can spend only three or four days aboard ship. On the other hand, Inside Passage–Gulf of Alaska cruises allow you to spend a full week aboard ship and still take a pre- or post-cruise land tour. A few lines schedule longer one-way or round-trip sailings from Vancouver, San Francisco, or Los Angeles.

Whether you sail through the Inside Passage or along it will depend on the size of your vessel. Smaller ships can navigate narrow channels, straits, and fjords. Larger vessels must sail farther from land, so don't expect to see much wildlife from the deck of a megaship.

Cruise Tours

Most cruise lines give you the option of an independent, hosted, or fully escorted land tour before or after your cruise. Independent tours allow maximum flexibility. You have a preplanned itinerary with confirmed hotel reservations and transportation arrangements, but you're free to follow your interests and whims in each town. A hosted tour is similar, but tour company representatives are available along the route to help out should you need assistance.

On fully escorted tours, you travel with a group, led by a tour director. Activities are preplanned (and typically prepaid), so you have a good idea of how much your trip will cost (not counting incidentals) before you depart.

Modes of tour transportation range from plane to bus, rail to ferry. Most cruise-tour itineraries include a ride aboard the Alaska Railroad in a glass-dome railcar. Running between Anchorage, Denali National Park, and Fairbanks, Holland America Westours' *McKinley Explorer* and Princess Tours' *Midnight Sun Express Ultra Dome* offer unobstructed views of the passing land and wildlife from private railcars.

Of the ocean-liner fleet, only the *Vision of the Seas, Rhapsody of the Seas, Universe Explorer, Norwegian Sky,* and

Norwegian Wind are not currently offering cruise-tour packages with land segments in Alaska; they may, however, have tours in the Canadian Rockies. In addition to full-length cruise tours, many cruise lines have pre- or post-cruise hotel and sightseeing packages in Vancouver or Anchorage lasting one to three days.

Cruise Costs

Per diems (*see* Chapter 4) are an average daily price for Alaska itineraries during peak season, based on published brochure rates: if you shop around and book early you will undoubtedly pay less. In addition to your cruise per diem are extra costs, such as **airfare** to the port city. Only the most expensive Alaska cruises include airfare. Virtually all lines offer air add-ons, which may or may not be less expensive than the latest discounted fare from the airlines.

Shore excursions can be a substantial expense; the best in Alaska are not cheap. But, skimp too much on your excursion budget and you'll deprive yourself of an important part of the Alaska experience.

Tipping is another extra. At the end of the cruise, it's customary to tip your room steward, server, and the person who buses your table. Expect to pay an average of $7.50 to $10 per day in tips. Each ship offers guidelines.

Single travelers should be aware that there are few single cabins on most ships; taking a double cabin for yourself can cost as much as twice the advertised per-person rates (which are based on two people sharing a room). Some cruise lines will find roommates of the same sex for singles so that each can travel at the regular per-person, double-occupancy rate.

When to Go

Cruise season runs from mid-May to late September; the most popular sailing dates are from late June through August. Although Alaskan weather never carries any guarantees, sunshine and warm days are apt to be most plentiful from mid-June through August. May and June are the driest months to cruise. For shoppers, bargains can be found both early and late in the season.

Cruising in the low seasons provides plenty of advantages besides discounted fares. Availability of ships and particular cabins is greater in the low and shoulder seasons, and the ports are almost completely free of tourists. In spring, wildflowers are abundant, and you're apt to see more wildlife along the shore because the animals have not yet gone up to higher elevations. Alaska's early fall brings the splendor of autumn hues and the first snowfalls in the mountains. The animals have returned to low ground, and shorter days bring the possibility of seeing the northern lights. Daytime temperatures along the cruise routes in May, June, and September are in the 50s and 60s. July and August averages are in the 60s and 70s, with occasional days in the 80s.

November is the best month for off-season ferry travel, after the stormy month of October and while it's still relatively warm on the Inside Passage (temperatures will average about 40 degrees). It's a good month for wildlife watching as well. Some animals show themselves in greater numbers during November. In particular, humpback whales are abundant off Sitka, and bald eagles congregate by the thousands near Haines.

BEFORE YOU GO

Tickets and Vouchers

After you make the final payment for your cruise, the cruise line will issue your cruise tickets and vouchers for airport–ship transfers. Depending on the airline, and whether you have purchased an air-sea package, you may receive your plane tickets or charter-flight vouchers at the same time; you may also receive vouchers for any shore excursions, although most cruise lines issue these aboard ship. Should your travel documents not arrive when promised, contact your travel agent or call the cruise line directly. If you book late, tickets may be delivered directly to the ship.

What to Pack

Certain packing rules apply to all cruises: always take along a sweater to counter cool evening ocean breezes or overactive air-conditioning. A rain slicker usually comes in handy, too, and make sure you take at least one pair of comfortable walking shoes for exploring port towns. No two cruises have quite the same dress policy, but evening dress on Alaskan cruises tends to fall into two categories: semiformal on the ocean liners and casual on the smaller ships. On semiformal cruises men generally wear a jacket and tie to dinner. Women should pack one long gown or cocktail dress for every two or three formal evenings on board. On smaller cruises, shipboard dress is usually informal.

Generally speaking, plan on one outfit for every two days of cruising, especially if your wardrobe contains many interchangeable pieces. Ships often have convenient laundry facilities as well. Don't overload your luggage with extra toiletries and sundry items; they are easily available in port and in the ship's gift shop (though usually at a premium price). Soaps, and sometimes shampoos and body lotion, are often placed in your cabin compliments of the cruise line.

Take an extra pair of eyeglasses or contact lenses in your carry-on luggage. If you have a health problem that requires a prescription drug, pack enough to last the duration of the trip or have your doctor write a prescription using the drug's generic name, because brand names vary from country to country. Always carry prescription drugs in their original packaging to avoid problems with customs officials. Don't pack them in luggage that you plan to check, in case your bags go astray. Pack a list of the offices that supply refunds for lost or stolen traveler's checks.

ARRIVING AND DEPARTING

If you have purchased an air-sea package, you will be met by a cruise-company representative when your plane lands at the port city and then shuttled directly to the ship in buses or minivans. Some cruise lines arrange to transport your luggage between airport and ship so you don't have to deal with baggage claim at the start of your cruise or with baggage check-in at the end. If you decide not to buy the air-sea package but still plan to fly, ask your travel agent if you can use the ship's transfer bus anyway; if you do, you may be required to purchase a round-trip transfer voucher (about $40). Otherwise, you will have to arrange for your own transportation to the ship.

Embarkation

Check-In
On arrival at the dock, you must check in before boarding your ship. A cruise-line official will collect or stamp your ticket, inspect or even retain your passport or other official identification, and give you the keys to your cabin. Seating assignments for the dining room are often handed out at this time, too.

After this you may be required to go through a security check and to pass your hand baggage through an X-ray inspection. These are the same machines in use at airports, so ask to have your photographic film inspected by hand.

Although it takes only five or ten minutes per family to check in, lines are often long, so aim to check in during off-peak hours. The worst time tends to be immediately after the ship begins boarding; the later it is, the less crowded. For example, if boarding begins at 2 PM and continues until 4:30, try to arrive after 3:30.

Boarding the Ship
You will be escorted to your cabin by a steward, who will carry your hand luggage. The rest of your bags will either be inside your cabin when you arrive or will come shortly thereafter. If your bags don't arrive within a half hour before sailing, contact the purser. If you are among the unlucky few whose luggage doesn't make it to the ship in time, the purser will trace it and arrange to have it flown to the next port of call.

Disembarkation

The last night of your cruise is full of business. On most ships you must place everything except your hand luggage outside your cabin door, ready to be picked up by midnight. Color-coded tags, distributed to your cabin in a debarkation packet, should be placed on your luggage before the crew collects it. Your designated color will later determine when you leave the ship and help you retrieve your luggage on the pier.

Your shipboard bill is left in your room during the last day; to pay the bill (if you haven't already put it on your credit card) or to settle any questions, you must stand in line at the purser's office. Tips to the cabin steward and dining staff are distributed on the last night.

The next morning, in-room breakfast service is usually not available because stewards are too busy. Most passengers clear out of their cabins as soon as possible, gather their hand luggage, and stake out a chair in one of the public lounges to await the ship's clearance through customs. Be patient—it takes a long time to unload and sort thousands of pieces of luggage. Passengers disembark by groups according to the color-coded tags placed on luggage the night before; those with the earliest flights get off first. If you have a tight connection, notify the purser before the last day, and he or she may be able to arrange faster preclearing and debarkation for you.

ON BOARD

Checking Out Your Cabin

The first thing to do upon arriving at your cabin or suite is to make sure that everything is in order. If there are two twin beds instead of the double bed you wanted, or other problems, ask to be moved *before* the ship departs. Unless the ship is full, you can usually persuade the chief housekeeper or hotel manager to allow you to change cabins. It is customary to tip the stewards who help you move.

Since your cabin is your home away from home for a few days or weeks, everything should be to your satisfaction. Take a good look around: Is the cabin clean and orderly? Do the toilet, shower, and faucets work? Check the telephone and television. Again, major problems should be addressed immediately. Minor concerns, such as a shortage of pillows, can wait until the frenzy of embarkation subsides.

Your dining-time and seating-assignment card may be in your cabin; now is the time to check it and immediately request any changes. The maître d' usually sets up shop in one of the public rooms specifically for this purpose.

Shipboard Accounts

Virtually all cruise ships operate as cashless societies. Passengers charge on-board purchases and settle their accounts at the end of the cruise with a credit card, traveler's checks, or cash. You can sign for wine at dinner, drinks at the bar, shore excursions, gifts in the shop—virtually any expense you may incur aboard ship. On some lines, an imprint from a major credit card is necessary to open an account. Otherwise, a cash deposit may be required and a positive balance maintained to keep the shipboard account open. Either way, you will want to open a line of credit soon after settling in if an account was not opened for you at embarkation. This can easily be arranged by visiting the purser's office in the central atrium or main lobby.

Tipping

For better or worse, tipping is an integral part of the cruise experience. Most companies pay their cruise staff nominal wages and expect tips to make up the difference. Cruise lines usually have recommended tipping guidelines, and on many ships voluntary tipping for beverage service has been replaced with a mandatory 15% service charge, which is added to every bar bill. On the other hand, the most expensive luxury lines include tipping in the cruise fare and may prohibit crew members from accepting any additional gratuities. On most small adventure ships, a collection box is placed in the dining room or lounge on the last full day of the cruise, and passengers contribute anonymously.

Dining

Ocean liners serve food nearly around the clock. There may be up to four breakfast options: early-morning coffee and pastries on deck, breakfast in bed through room service, buffet-style in the cafeteria, and sit-down in the dining room. There may also be several lunch choices, mid-afternoon hors d'oeuvres, and midnight buffets. You can eat whatever is on the menu, in any quantity, at as many of these meals as you wish. Room service is traditionally, but not always, free (*see* Shipboard Services, *below*).

Restaurants

The chief meals of the day are served in the main dining room, which on most ships can accommodate only half the passengers at once. Meals are therefore usually served in two sittings—early (or main) and late (or second) seating. Early seating for dinner is generally between 6 and 6:30, late seating between 8 and 8:30.

Most cruise ships have a cafeteria-style restaurant, usually near the swimming pool, where you can eat lunch and breakfast (dinner is usually served only in the dining room). Many ships provide self-serve coffee or tea in their cafeteria around the clock, as well as buffets at midnight.

Increasingly, ships also have alternative restaurants, usually serving Italian food. These are found mostly on newer vessels, although some older liners have been refitted for alternative dining. Other ships have pizzerias, ice-cream parlors, and caviar or cappuccino bars; there may be an extra charge at these facilities.

Smoking policies vary, but more lines are banning smoking in their main dining rooms. Contact your cruise line to find out what the situation will be on your cruise.

Seatings

When it comes to your dining-table assignment, you should have options on four important points: early or late seating; smoking or no-smoking section (if smoking is allowed in the dining room); a table for two, four, six, or eight; and special dietary needs. When you receive your cruise documents, you will usually receive a card asking for your dining preferences. Fill this out and return it to the cruise line, but remember that you will not get your seating assignment until you board the ship. Check it out immediately, and if your request was not met, see the maître d'—usually there is a time and place set up for changes in dining assignments.

On some ships, seating times are strictly observed. Ten to 15 minutes after the scheduled mealtime, the dining-room doors are closed. On other ships, passengers may enter the dining room at their leisure, but they must be out by the end of the seating. When a ship has just one seating, passengers may enter at any time while the kitchen is open.

Seating assignments on some ships apply only for dinner. Several have open seating for breakfast or lunch, which means you may sit anywhere at any time. Smaller or more luxurious ships offer open seating for all meals.

CHANGING TABLES

Dining is a focal point of the cruise experience, and your companions at meals may become your best friends on the cruise. However, if you don't enjoy the company at your table, the maître d' can usually move you to another one if the dining room isn't completely full—a tip helps. He will probably be reluctant to comply with your request after the first full day at sea, however, because the waiters, busboys, and wine steward who have been serving you up to that point won't receive their tips at the end of the cruise. Be persistent if you are truly unhappy.

Cuisine

Aboard all cruise ships the quality of the cooking is generally good, but even a skilled chef is hard put to serve 500 or more extraordinary dinners per hour. But the presentation is often spectacular, especially at gala midnight buffets.

There is a direct relationship between the cost of a cruise and the quality of its cuisine. The food is very sophisticated on some (mostly expensive) lines, among them Crystal Cruises. In the more moderate price range, Celebrity Cruises has gained renown for the culinary stylings of French chef Michel Roux, who acts as a consultant to the line.

Special Diets

With notification well in advance, many ships can provide a kosher, low-salt, low-cholesterol, sugar-free, vegetarian, or other special menu. However, there's always a chance that the wrong dish will somehow be handed to you. Especially when it comes to soups and desserts, it's a good idea to ask about the ingredients.

Large ships usually offer an alternative "light" or "spa" menu based upon American Heart Association guidelines, using less fat, leaner cuts of meat, low-cholesterol or low-sodium preparations, smaller portions, salads, fresh-fruit desserts, and healthy garnishes. Some smaller ships may not be able to accommodate special dietary needs. Vegetarians generally have no trouble finding appropriate selections.

Wine

Wine at meals costs extra on most ships; the prices are usually comparable to those in shoreside restaurants and are charged to your shipboard account. A handful of luxury vessels include both wine and liquor.

The Captain's Table

It is both a privilege and a marvelous experience to be invited to dine one evening at the captain's table. Although some seats are given to celebrities, repeat passengers, and passengers in the most expensive suites, other invitations are given at random to ordinary passengers. You can request an invitation from the chief steward or the hotel manager, although there is no guarantee you will be accommodated. The captain's guests always wear a suit and tie or a dress, even if the dress code for that evening is casual. On many ships, passengers may also be invited to dine at the other officers' special tables, or officers may visit a different passenger table each evening.

Entertainment

Lounges and Nightclubs

On ocean liners, the main entertainment lounge or show-room schedules nightly musical revues, magic acts, comedy performances, and variety shows. During the rest of the day the room is used for group activities, such as shore-excursion talks or bingo games. Generally, the larger the ship the bigger and more impressive the productions. Newer ships have elaborate showrooms that often span two decks. Some are designed like an amphitheater while others have two levels—a main floor and a balcony. Seating is sometimes in clusters of armchairs set around cocktail tables. Other ships have more traditional theater-style seating.

Many larger ships have a second showroom. Entertainment and ballroom dancing may go on here late into the night. Elsewhere you may find a disco, nightclub, or cabaret, usually built around a bar and dance floor. Music is provided by a piano player, a disc jockey, or by performing ensembles such as country-and-western duos or jazz combos.

On smaller ships the entertainment options are more limited, sometimes consisting of no more than a piano around which passengers gather. There may be a main lounge where scaled-down revues are staged.

Bars

A ship's bars, whether adjacent to the pool or attached to one of the lounges, tend to be its social centers. Except on a handful of luxury-class ships where everything is included in the ticket price, bars operate on a pay-as-it's-poured basis. Rather than demand cash after every round, however, most ships allow you to charge drinks to an account.

In international waters there are, technically, no laws against teenage drinking, but almost all ships require passengers to be over 18 or 21 to purchase alcoholic drinks. Many cruise ships have chapters of Alcoholics Anonymous (a.k.a. "Friends of Bill W.") or will organize meetings on request. Look for meeting times and places in the daily program slipped under your cabin door each night.

Library

Most cruise ships have a library with up to 1,500 volumes, from the latest best-sellers to reference works. Many shipboard libraries also stock videotapes for those cabins with VCRs.

Movie Theaters

All but the smallest vessels have a room for screening movies. On older ships and some newer ones, this is often a genuine cinema-style movie theater. On other ships, it may be just a multipurpose room. The films are frequently one or two months past their first release date but not yet available on videotape or cable TV. Films rated "R" are edited to minimize sex and violence. On a weeklong voyage, a dozen different films may be screened, each one repeated at various times during the day. Theaters are also used for lectures, religious services, and private meetings.

With a few exceptions, ocean liners equip their cabins with closed-circuit TVs; these show movies (continuously on some newer ships), shipboard lectures, and regular programs (thanks to satellite reception). Ships with VCRs in the cabins usually provide a selection of movies on at no charge (a deposit is sometimes required).

Casinos

Once a ship is 12 mi off American shores, it is in international waters and gambling is permitted. All ocean liners have casinos with poker, baccarat, blackjack, roulette, craps, and slot machines. House stakes are much more modest than those in Las Vegas or Atlantic City. On most ships the maximum bet is $200; some ships allow $500. Payouts on the slot machines (some of which take as little as a nickel) are generally much lower, too. Credit is never extended, but many casinos have handy credit-card machines that dispense cash for a hefty fee.

Most ships offer free individual instruction and even gambling classes in the off hours. Casinos are usually open from early morning until late at night, although you may find only unattended slot machines before evening. In accordance with local laws, casinos are always closed while a ship is in port. Officially, children are barred from the casinos, but it's common to see them playing the slots rather than the adjacent video machines.

Game Rooms

Most ships have a game or card room with card tables and board games. These rooms are for serious players and are often the setting for friendly round-robin competitions and tournaments. Most ships furnish everything for free (cards, chips, games, and so forth), but a few charge $1 or more for each deck of cards. Be aware that professional cardsharps and hustlers have been fleecing ship passengers almost as long as there have been ships. There are small video arcades on most medium and large ships. Family-oriented ships often have a computer learning center as well.

Bingo and Other Games

The daily high-stakes bingo games are even more popular than the casinos. You can play for as little as a dollar a card. Most ships have a snowball bingo game with a jackpot that grows throughout the cruise into hundreds or even thousands of dollars. Another popular cruise pastime is so-called "horse races": fictional horses are auctioned off to "owners." Individual passengers can buy a horse or form "syndicates." Bids usually begin at around $25 and can top $1,000 per horse. Races are then "run" according to dice throws or computer-generated random numbers. Audience members bet on their favorites.

Sports and Fitness

Swimming Pools

All but the smallest ships have at least one pool, some of them elaborate affairs with water slides or retractable roofs; hot tubs and whirlpools are quite common. Pools may be filled with fresh water or saltwater; some ships have one of each. While in port or during rough weather, the pools are usually emptied or covered with canvas. Many are too narrow or too short to allow swimmers more than a few strokes in any direction; none have diving boards, and not all are heated. Often there are no lifeguards. Wading pools are sometimes provided for small children.

Sun Deck

The top deck is usually called the Sun Deck or Sports Deck. On some ships this is where you'll find the pool or whirlpool; on others it is dedicated to volleyball, table tennis, shuffleboard, and other sports. A number of ships have paddle-tennis courts, and a few have golf driving ranges. Often, after the sun goes down, the Sun Deck is used for dancing, barbecues, or other social activities.

Exercise and Fitness Rooms

Most newer ships and some older ones have well-equipped fitness centers, many with massage, sauna, and whirlpools. An upper-deck fitness center often has an airy and sunny view of the sea; an inside, lower-deck health club is often dark and small unless it is equipped with an indoor pool or beauty salon. Many ships have full-service exercise rooms with bodybuilding and cardiovascular equipment, aerobics classes, and personal fitness instruction. Some ships even have cruise-length physical-fitness programs, which may include lectures on weight loss or nutrition. These often are tied in with a spa menu in the dining room. Beauty salons adjacent to the health club may offer spa treatments such as facials and mud wraps. The more extensive programs are often sold on a daily or weekly basis.

Promenade Deck

Many vessels designate certain decks for fitness walks and may post the number of laps per mile. Fitness instructors sometimes lead daily walks around the Promenade Deck. A number of ships discourage jogging and running on the decks or ask that no one take fitness walks before 8 AM or after 10 PM, so as not to disturb passengers in cabins. With the advent of the megaship, walking and jogging have in many cases moved up top to tracks on the Sun or Sports deck.

Shipboard Services

Room Service

A small number of ships have no room service at all, except when the ship's doctor orders it for an ailing passenger. Many offer only breakfast (Continental on some, full on others), while others provide no more than a limited menu at certain hours of the day. Most, however, have selections that you can order at any time. Some luxury ships have unlimited round-the-clock room service. There is usually no charge other than for beer, wine, or spirits.

Minibars

An increasing number of ships equip their more expensive cabins with small refrigerators or minibars stocked with snacks, soda, and liquors, which may or may not be free.

Laundry and Dry Cleaning

All but the smallest ships and shortest cruises offer laundry services—full-service, self-service, or both. Use of machines is generally free, although some ships charge for detergent or use of the machines or both. Valet laundry service includes cabin pickup and delivery and usually takes 24 hours. Most ships also offer dry-cleaning services.

Hair Stylists

Even the smallest ships have a hair stylist on staff. Larger ships have complete beauty salons, and some have barbershops. Book your appointment well in advance, especially before popular events like the farewell dinner.

Film Processing

Many ships have color-film processing equipment to develop film overnight. It's expensive but convenient.

Photographer

The staff photographer, a near-universal fixture on cruise ships, records every memorable, photogenic moment. The thousands of photos snapped over the course of a cruise are displayed publicly in special cases every morning and are offered for sale, usually for $6 for a 5″ × 7″ color print or $12 for an 8″ × 10″. If you want a special photo or a portrait, the photographer is usually happy to oblige. Many passengers choose to have a formal portrait taken before the captain's farewell dinner—the dressiest evening of the cruise. The ship's photographer usually sets up a studio near the dining-room entrance.

Religious Services

Most ships provide nondenominational religious services on Sundays and religious holidays, and a number offer Catholic masses daily and Jewish services on Friday evenings. The kind of service held depends upon the clergy the cruise line invites on board. Usually religious services are held in the library, the theater, or one of the private lounges, although a few ships have actual chapels.

Communications

SHIPBOARD

Most cabins have loudspeakers and telephones. Generally, the loudspeakers cannot be switched off because they are needed to broadcast important notices. Telephones are used to call fellow passengers, order room service, summon a doctor, request a wake-up call, or speak with any of the ship's officers or departments.

SHIP TO SHORE

Satellite facilities make it possible to call anywhere in the world from most ships. Most are also equipped with telex and fax machines, and some provide credit card–operated phones. It may take as long as a half hour to make a connection, but unless a storm is raging outside, conversation is clear and easy. On older ships, voice calls must be put through on shortwave wireless or via the one phone in the radio room. Newer ships are generally equipped with direct-dial phones in every cabin for calls to shore. Be warned: the cost of sending any message, regardless of the method, can be expensive—anywhere from $4–$15 a minute. If possible, wait until you go ashore to call home.

SAFETY AT SEA

Fire Safety

The greatest danger facing cruise-ship passengers is fire. All of the ships reviewed in this book must meet certain international fire-safety standards. The latest rules require that ships have sprinkler systems, smoke detectors, and other safety features. However, these rules are designed to protect against loss of life. They do not guarantee that a fire will not happen; in fact, fire is relatively common on cruise ships. The point here is not to create alarm, but to emphasize the importance of taking fire safety seriously.

Once you've settled into your cabin, find the location of the life vests and review the emergency instructions inside the cabin door or near the life vests. Make sure your vests are in good condition and learn to secure them properly. If you are traveling with children, be sure that child-size life jackets are placed in your cabin. Let the ship's purser know if you have a disability that may hamper a speedy exit from your cabin. In case of a real emergency, the purser can quickly dispatch a crew member to assist you.

Within 24 hours of embarkation, you will be asked to attend a mandatory lifeboat drill. Do so and listen carefully. If you have any questions, ask them. If you are unsure how to use your vest, now is the time to ask. Only in the most extreme circumstances will you need to abandon ship—but it has happened. The few minutes you spend learning the right procedure may serve you well in the rare event of a mishap.

Health Care

All big ships are equipped with infirmaries to handle minor emergencies. There are no international standards governing medical facilities or personnel aboard cruise ships, although the American Medical Association has recommended that such standards be adopted. If you have a pre-existing medical condition, discuss your upcoming cruise with your doctor. Pack an extra supply of any medicines you might need. Once aboard, alert the ship's doctor to your condition, and discuss treatments or emergency procedures before any problem arises. Passengers with potentially life-threatening conditions should seriously consider signing up with a medical-evacuation service. Review your health insurance to make sure you are covered while on a cruise.

The most common minor medical problems confronting cruise passengers are seasickness and gastrointestinal distress. Modern cruise ships, unlike their transatlantic predecessors, are relatively motion-free vessels with computer-controlled stabilizers, and they usually sail in relatively calm waters. If you do feel queasy, you can always get seasickness pills aboard ship. (Many ships give them out for free at the front desk.)

Outbreaks of food poisoning happen from time to time aboard cruise ships. Episodes are random; they can occur on ships old and new, big and small, budget and luxury. The Centers for Disease Control and Prevention (CDC) monitors cruise-ship hygiene and sanitation procedures, conducting voluntary inspections twice a year of all ships that sail regularly from U.S. ports (this program does not include ships that never visit the United States). For a free listing of the latest ship scores, write the CDC's National Center for Environmental Health (Vessel Sanitation Program, 1015 North America Way, Room 107, Miami, FL 33132). You can also get a copy from the CDC's fax-back service at 888/232–3299. Request publication 510051. Another alternative is to visit the Centers' Web site at www.cdc.gov.

Be aware that a high score on the CDC report doesn't necessarily mean a food-poisoning outbreak won't occur. Outbreaks have taken place on ships that consistently score very highly; conversely, some ships score very poorly yet passengers never get sick. So use these scores as a guideline and factor them in with other considerations when choosing your ship.

Crime on Ships

Crime aboard cruise ships has gained some attention recently, thanks in large part to a few well-publicized cases. Most people never have any type of problem, but you should exercise the same precautions aboard ship that you would at home. Keep your valuables out of sight—on big ships virtually every cabin has a small safe in the closet. Don't carry too much cash ashore; use your credit card whenever possible; and keep your money in a secure place, such as a front pocket, which is harder to pick than a back pocket. Single women traveling with friends should stick together, especially when returning to their cabins late at night. And be careful about whom you befriend, as you would anywhere, whether it's a fellow passenger or a member of the crew. You may be on vacation, but criminals rarely take a holiday. Don't be paranoid, but do be prudent.

GOING ASHORE

Traveling by cruise ship presents an opportunity to visit many different places in a short time. The flip side is that your stay will be limited in each port of call. For that reason, cruise lines arrange shore excursions, which maximize passengers' time by organizing their touring for them. There are a number of advantages to shore excursions: in some destinations, transportation may be unreliable, and a ship-package tour is the best way to see distant sights. Also, you don't have to worry about being stranded or missing the ship. The disadvantage is that you will pay more for the convenience of having the ship do the legwork for you. Of course, you can always book a tour independently, hire a taxi, or use foot power to explore on your own.

Information on local tours is available at the visitor-information counter in each port. The counter is usually close to the pier. For exact locations, *see* Coming Ashore *in each port of call section in* Chapter 2.

Arriving in Port

When your ship arrives in a port, it will either tie up alongside a dock or anchor out in a harbor. If the ship is docked, passengers walk down the gangway to go ashore. Docking makes it easy to go back and forth between the shore and the ship.

Tendering

If your ship anchors in the harbor, however, you will have to take a small boat—called a launch or tender—to get ashore. Tendering is a nuisance. When your ship first arrives in port, everyone wants to go ashore. Often, in order to avoid a stampede at the tenders, you must gather in a public room, get a boarding pass, and wait up to a half hour until your number is called. This continues until everybody has disembarked. Even then, it may take 15–20 minutes to get ashore if your ship is anchored far offshore. Because tenders can be difficult to board, passengers with mobility problems may not be able to visit certain ports. The larger the ship, the more likely that it will use tenders. It is usually possible to learn before booking a cruise whether the ship will dock or anchor at its ports of call. (For more information about where ships dock, tender, or both, *see* Chapter 2.)

Before anyone is allowed to walk down the gangway or board a tender, the ship must first be cleared for landing. Immigration and customs officials board the vessel to examine passports and sort through red tape. It may be more than an hour before you're actually allowed ashore. You will be issued a boarding pass, which you will need to get back on board.

Returning to the Ship

Cruise lines are strict about sailing times, which are posted at the gangway and elsewhere and announced in the daily schedule of activities. Be certain to be back on board at least half an hour before the announced sailing time or you may be stranded. If you are on a shore excursion that was sold by the cruise line, however, the captain will wait for your group before casting off. That is one reason many passengers prefer ship-packaged tours.

If you are not on one of the ship's tours and the ship does sail without you, immediately contact the cruise line's port representative, whose name and phone number is often listed on the daily schedule of activities. You may be able to hitch a ride on a pilot boat, though that is unlikely. Passengers who miss the boat must pay their own way to the next port of call.

2 Ports of Call

Nearly every day, your ship will make a port call. Visiting port cities allows you to explore the culture, wildlife, history, and amazing scenery that make Alaska so unique. Alaskan port cities are small and easily explored on foot, but for those who prefer to be shown the sights, ship-organized shore excursions are available (*see* Chapter 3). These range from typical city bus tours to flightseeing with a landing on a glacier, charter fishing, river rafting, or visiting Native communities.

Dining

Not surprisingly, seafood dominates most menus. In summer, salmon, halibut, crab, cod, and prawns are usually fresh. Restaurants are informal and casual clothes are the norm; you'll never be sent away for wearing jeans to an Alaskan restaurant.

CATEGORY	COST*
$$$	over $40
$$	$20–$40
$	under $20

per person for a three-course meal, excluding drinks, service, and sales tax

Saloons

Socializing at a bar or saloon is an old Alaska custom, and the towns and cities of the Southeast Panhandle are no exception. Listed under the individual ports of call are some of the favorite gathering places in these parts.

Sea Kayaking

More adventurous travelers will enjoy paddling sea kayaks in the protected waters of Southeast and South Central Alaska. Ketchikan, Homer, Juneau, Seward, Sitka, and Valdez all have companies that rent sea kayaks, with lessons and short kayak tours available. Gear is usually provided.

Shopping

Alaskan Native handicrafts range from Tlingit totem poles—a few inches high to several feet tall—to Athabascan beaded slippers and fur garments. Many other traditional pieces of art are found in gift shops up and down the coast: Inupiat spirit masks, Yupik dolls and dance fans, Tlingit button blankets and silver jewelry, and Aleut grass baskets and carved wooden items. To ensure authenticity, buy items tagged with the state-approved AUTHENTIC NATIVE HAND-

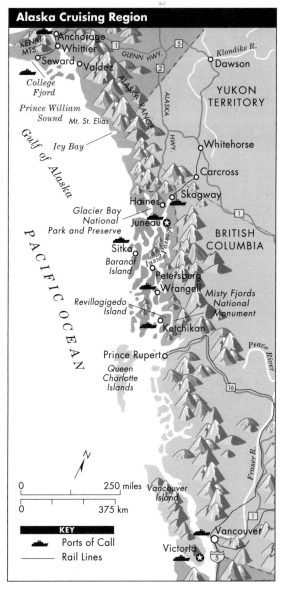

Alaska Cruising Region

KENAI MTS.
Anchorage
Whittier
Seward
Valdez
College Fjord
Prince William Sound
GLENN HWY.
ALASKA RANGE
Mt. St. Elias
Icy Bay
Gulf of Alaska
ALASKA HWY.
Klondike R.
Dawson
YUKON TERRITORY
Whitehorse
Carcross
Haines
Skagway
Glacier Bay National Park and Preserve
Juneau
Sitka
Baranof Island
Inside Passage
BRITISH COLUMBIA
Petersburg
Wrangell
Misty Fjords National Monument
Revillagigedo Island
Ketchikan
Prince Rupert
Queen Charlotte Islands
Peace River
PACIFIC OCEAN
Fraser R.
Vancouver Island
Vancouver
Victoria

0   250 miles
0   375 km

KEY
Ports of Call
Rail Lines

CRAFT FROM ALASKA "Silverhand" label. Better prices are found in the more remote villages where you buy directly from the artisan, in museum shops, or in craft fairs such as Anchorage's downtown Saturday Market.

Salmon, halibut, crab, and other seafood are very popular with both locals and visitors. Most towns have a local company that packs and ships seafood.

Anchorage

Nearly half of all Alaskans live in Anchorage, the state's only true metropolis. Visitors will discover a flower-filled downtown, fine restaurants, and a wide range of attractions—both natural and human—in the area. Despite all its cosmopolitan trappings, this city of 258,000 people maintains something of an opportunistic, pioneer spirit. Its inhabitants hustle for their living in the oil, retail, transportation, communications, government, banking, medical, and education fields.

Superficially, Anchorage looks like any other sprawling western American city, with Wal-Marts and shopping malls, but sled-dog races are as popular here as surfing is in California, and moose occasionally roam along city bike trails. This is basically a modern, relatively unattractive city, but the Chugach Mountains form a striking backdrop, and spectacular Alaskan wilderness is found just outside the back door. Few people come to Alaska to see Anchorage, but most pass through at some time during their trip, and the city does have almost anything you may want, from Starbucks espresso to Native handicrafts.

Anchorage took shape with the construction of the federally funded Alaska Railroad (completed in 1923), and traces of the city's railroad heritage remain. With the tracks laid, the town's pioneer settlers actively sought expansion by hook and—not infrequently—by crook. City founders, some of whom are still alive, delight in telling how they tricked a visiting U.S. congressman into dedicating the site for a federal hospital that had not yet been approved.

Boom and bust periods followed major events: an influx of military bases during World War II; a massive buildup of Arctic missile-warning stations early in the Cold War; and, more recently, the discovery of oil at Prudhoe Bay and the construction of the trans-Alaska pipeline.

Anchorage today is Alaska at its most urban. There's a performing-arts center, a diversity of museums, and a variety of ethnic eateries for cruise passengers to sample.

Several establishments that are only open in the evening are listed here because cruise-ship passengers frequently stay overnight in Anchorage.

Coming Ashore

Cruise ships visiting Anchorage most often dock at the port city of Seward, 125 mi to the south on the Kenai Peninsula; from here passengers must travel by bus (three hours) or train (four hours) to Anchorage. The train station is a few blocks away from downtown Anchorage. Ships that do sail directly to the city dock just beyond downtown. There is a tourist-information booth on the pier. The major attractions are a 15- or 20-minute walk away; turn right when you disembark and head south on Ocean Dock Road. The main tourist district of downtown Anchorage is easy to navigate on foot. If you want to see some of the outlying attractions, like Lake Hood (*see* Exploring, *below*), you'll need to hire a taxi. Taxis are expensive: rates start at $2 for pickup and $2 for each mile (1½ km). Most people in Anchorage telephone for a cab, although it is possible to hail one downtown. Contact **Alaska Cab** (tel. 907/563–5353), **Anchorage Taxicab** (tel. 907/278–8000), **Checker Cab** (tel. 907/276–1234), or **Yellow Cab** (tel. 907/272–2422).

If you have the time and want to explore sites farther afield, such as Girdwood and points south on the Kenai Peninsula, Anchorage is a great place to rent a car. **National Car Rental** has a downtown office (1300 E. 5th Ave., tel. 907/265–7553). Major rental companies all have airport desks and provide free shuttle service to the airport to pick up cars. Agencies with airport desks include **Affordable New Car Rental** (tel. 907/243–3370), **Arctic Rent-a-Car** (tel. 907/561–2990), **Budget** (tel. 907/243– 0150), and **Denali Car Rental** (tel. 907/276-1230).

Exploring Anchorage

Numbers in the margin correspond to points of interest on the Downtown Anchorage map.

❶ A marker in front of the **Log Cabin Visitor Information Center** shows the mileage to various world cities. Fourth Avenue sustained heavy damage in the massive 1964 earthquake. The businesses on this block withstood the destruction, but those a block east fell into the ground as the earth under them slid toward Ship Creek. *Corner of 4th Ave. and F St., tel. 907/274– 3531. Open summer, daily 7:30–7; spring and fall, daily 8–6.*

Anchorage's real centerpiece is its distinctively modern **❷** **Performing Arts Center** (tel. 907/263–2900) at 5th Ave. and G Street. A diversity of musical, theatrical, and dance groups perform here throughout the year. Out front is flower-packed **Town Square,** a delightful place to relax on a sunny day.

❸ The Art Deco **Fourth Avenue Theater** (4th Ave. between F and G streets) has been restored and put to new use as a gift shop, café, and gallery. Note the lighted stars in the ceiling that form the Big Dipper against a field of blue—it's the design of the Alaska state flag.

Displays about Alaska's national parks, forests, and wildlife **❹** refuges can be seen at the **Alaska Public Lands Information Center.** The center also shows films highlighting different regions of the state and sells natural history books. *4th Ave. and F St., tel. 907/271–2737. Open daily 9–5:30 in summer.*

❺ **Resolution Park,** a cantilevered viewing platform dominated by a monument to British explorer Captain Cook, looks out toward Cook Inlet and the mountains beyond. Mt. Susitna (known as the Sleeping Lady) is the prominent low mountain to the northwest. To her north, Mt. McKinley is often visible 125 mi away. (Most Alaskans prefer the traditional name for this peak, Denali.)

The paved **Tony Knowles Coastal Trail** runs along Cook Inlet for about 11 mi (18 km), and is accessible from the west end of 2nd Avenue. This is a wonderful place to take in the view, or to join the throngs of folks walking, running, biking, or rollerblading.

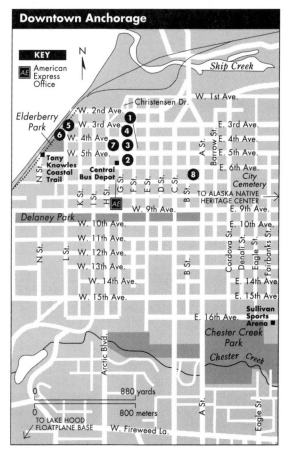

Downtown Anchorage

KEY

AE American Express Office

Alaska Public Lands Information Center, **4**

Anchorage Museum of History and Art, **8**

Fourth Avenue Theater, **3**

Imaginarium, **7**

Log Cabin Visitor Information Center, **1**

Oscar Anderson House, **6**

Performing Arts Center, **2**

Resolution Park, **5**

❻ The **Oscar Anderson House,** next to the trail at the north end of Elderberry Park, was Anchorage's first permanent frame house, built in 1915. Tours are free. In late summer the park is also a good place to watch for porpoise-size beluga whales in Cook Inlet. *Near 5th Ave. between L and N Sts., tel. 907/274–2336. Admission: $3. Open Tues.–Sat. noon–4.*

❼ A fun stop for kids and adults alike is the **Imaginarium,** an interactive science museum that lets kids stand inside a giant soap bubble, hold a starfish in the marine exhibit, or take a galaxy tour in the planetarium. There's also a great gift shop. *725 W. 5th Ave., tel. 907/276–3179. Admission: $5. Open Mon.– Sat. 10–6, Sun. noon–5.*

❽ The **Anchorage Museum of History and Art** occupies the whole block at 6th Avenue and A Street, with an entrance on 7th Avenue. It houses a fine collection of historical and contemporary Alaskan art, displays on Alaskan history, and a special section for children. One gallery is devoted to views of Alaska, as seen by early explorers, painters, and contemporary artists. *121 W. 7th Ave., tel. 907/343–4326. Admission: $5. Open daily 9–6.*

The new **Alaska Native Heritage Center** opened in 1999 on the northeast side of Anchorage. On a 26-acre site facing the Chugach Mountains, this $15-million dollar facility includes a spacious Welcome House, where you are introduced to the Native peoples of Alaska through displays, artifacts, photographs, demonstrations, performances, and films. Visitors then head outside to circle a small lake while exploring five village exhibits. At each of these you will see traditional structures and can watch Native peoples demonstrating their culture. A café and gift shop are here as well. *8800 Heritage Center Dr. (Glenn Hwy. at Muldoon Rd.), 5 mi east of downtown, tel. 907/330–8000. Admission: $20. Open daily 9–9.*

If you have the time, take a taxi to the **Lake Hood floatplane base,** where colorful aircraft come and go almost constantly in the summer months. The best vantage point is from the patio of the lounge at the Regal Alaskan Hotel (4800 Spenard Rd., tel. 907/243–2300).

Shopping

During the summer, Anchorage's **Saturday Market** fills the parking lot at 3rd Avenue and E Street; browse here for Alaskan-made crafts, fresh produce, and food. *Open Saturdays 9–6.*

Several downtown shops sell quality Native Alaskan artwork, but the best buys are at the gift shop inside the **Alaska Native Medical Center.** *Tudor Centre Dr. off East Tudor Rd., tel. 907/729–1122. Open weekdays 10–2, 1st Sat. of month 10–2.*

Artwork created by Alaskan artists, both Native and non-Native, can be found at **Artique Ltd.** (314 G St., tel. 907/277–1663). The work of better-known Alaskan artists can be seen at the **Decker/Morris Gallery** (corner of 7th Ave. and G St., in the Performing Arts Center, tel. 907/272–1489). For "wearable art" and one-of-a-kind designs in polar fleece apparel, stop in at designer **Tracy Anna Bader's** boutique (416 G St., tel. 907/272– 6668). Another option for warm wear is the **Oomingmak Musk Ox Producers Co-op** (corner of 6th Ave. and H St., tel. 907/272– 9225). Native Alaskan villagers hand knit scarves and hats from the soft-as-cashmere underwool of the musk ox into traditional designs. Another place for distinctive garments and parkas is **Laura Wright Alaskan Parkas** (343 W. 5th Ave., tel. 907/274– 4215). The parkas are available off-the-rack or by custom order. Not far from here is **Cook Inlet Book Company** (415 W. 5th Ave., tel. 907/258–4544), with a huge selection of Alaskan titles.

Wolf aficionados will enjoy a stop at **Wolf Song** (corner of 6th Ave. and C St., tel. 907/274–9653), a nonprofit gift shop with wildlife art and educational material. The **Alaska General Store** (715 W. 4th Ave., tel. 907/272–1672) gift shop is a browser's delight, with an old-fashioned ambience and a diverse collection of objects old and new.

Anchorage's best places to buy fresh, frozen, or smoked seafood are not far from the center of town: **10th and M Seafoods** (1020 M St., tel. 907/272–6013) and **New Sagaya's City Market** (900 W. 13th Ave., tel. 907/274– 6173). Both places will also ship seafood for you.

Entertainment

Take a goofy, off-kilter romp across Alaska at the "Whale Fat Follies" Tuesday through Saturday evenings in the **Fly By Night Club** (3300 Spenard Rd., tel. 907/279–7726). Mr. Whitekeys is the master of ceremonies for this musical extravaganza of bad taste and Spam jokes.

Sports

JOGGING/WALKING

The Tony Knowles Coastal Trail (*see* Exploring Anchorage, *above*) and other trails in Anchorage are used by cyclists, runners, and walkers. The trail from Westchester Lagoon at the end of 15th Avenue runs 2 mi (3 km) to Earthquake Park and, beyond that, 9 mi (15 km) out to Kincaid Park. For bike rentals, contact **Adventure Cafe** (414 K St., tel. 907/276–8282 or 800/288–3134) or **Downtown Bicycle Rental** (corner of 5th Ave. and C St., tel. 907/279– 5293).

Dining

$$–$$$ **Club Paris.** It's dark and smoky up front in the bar, where for decades old-time Anchorage folks have met to drink and chat. Alaskan seafood, salads, and sandwiches are available, but the star attractions are the big, tender, flavorful steaks. If you have to wait for a table, have a martini at the bar and order the hors d'oeuvres tray—a sampler of steak, cheese, and prawns that could be a meal for two people. *417 W. 5th Ave., tel. 907/277– 6332. AE, D, DC, MC, V.*

$$–$$$ **Marx Bros. Cafe.** Fusion cuisine served by chef Jack Amon shows that frontier cooking is much more than a kettle in the kitchen. Among the multicultural specialties of the house is baked halibut with a macadamia crust served with coconut curry and mango chutney. Reservations are essential—you might even want to call before you reach Anchorage. *627 W. 3rd Ave., tel. 907/278–2133. AE, DC, MC, V. No lunch.*

$$–$$$ **Sacks Cafe.** The downtown business crowd favors this bright little café. Delightfully creative soups, panini sandwiches, and salads fill the lunch menu, and for dinner the kitchen produces such entrées as lamb braised in a spicy red curry sauce and baked penne pasta with sun-dried tomatoes, spinach, roasted peppers, and three cheeses. Be sure to check out the extraordinary daily specials. The salads are large enough for a light meal, but be sure to leave room for dessert, especially the decadent chocolate gâteau. *625 W. 5th Ave., tel. 907/276–3546. AE, MC, V.*

$$–$$$ **Simon & Seafort's Saloon and Grill.** This is the place to enjoy a great view across Cook Inlet while dining on consistently fine Alaskan seafood or rock salt-roasted prime rib. The bar is a good spot for appetizers, including beer-batter halibut and potatoes Gorgonzola, but you can also order from the full menu. *Corner of 4th Ave. and L St., tel. 907/274–3502. AE, DC, MC, V.*

$–$$ **Thai Cuisine Too.** The menu here is a welcome change from Alaska's ubiquitous seafood and steak houses; you'll find all the Thai standards, including fresh rolls, pad-thai, and a wonderful tom khar gai soup. The food is dependably good, and the atmosphere is quiet and friendly. Thai Cuisine Too is right in the center of town and is especially popular for lunch. *328 G St., tel. 907/277–8424. AE, MC, V.*

BREW PUBS

Brew pubs, along with a multitude of espresso stands, have arrived in Anchorage:

Alaska Glacier Brew House Restaurant. Tasty food, such as wood-fired pizza, fresh seafood, and rotisserie-grilled meats, complements the home-brewed beer in a stylish setting with high ceilings, an open kitchen, and a central fireplace. *737 W. 5th Ave., tel. 907/274–2739. AE, DC, MC, V.*

Humpy's Great Alaskan Alehouse. This immensely popular restaurant and bar has more than 40 draft beers on tap and cranks out huge plates of halibut burgers, health-nut chicken, and smoked-salmon Caesar salad. Humpy's has live music most evenings, so don't expect quiet (or a smoke-free atmosphere) in this hopping nightspot. *610 W. 6th Ave., tel. 907/276–2337. AE, D, DC, MC, V.*

Snowgoose Restaurant and Sleeping Lady Brewing Company. This brew-pub is notable for its award-winning beers and large deck overlooking Cook Inlet, Mt. Susitna (the Sleeping Lady), and—on a clear day—Mt. McKinley. The menu includes pizzas, burgers, and pasta, along with seafood specials each evening. Unfortunately, smoke from the upstairs pub (where cigars are allowed) sometimes drifts down to patrons below. *717 W. 3rd Ave., tel. 907/277–7727. AE, MC, V.*

Glacier Bay National Park and Preserve

Cruising Glacier Bay is like revisiting the Little Ice Age, when glaciers covered much of the northern hemisphere. This is one of the few places in the world where you can get within a quarter mi (½ km) of tidewater glaciers, which have their base at the water's edge. Twelve of them line the 60 mi (96 km) of narrow fjords at the northern end of the Inside Passage. Huge chunks of ice break off the glaciers and crash into the water, producing a dazzling show known as calving.

Although the Tlingit have lived in the area for 10,000 years, the bay was first popularized by naturalist John Muir, who visited in 1879. Just 100 years before, the bay was completely choked with ice. By 1916, though, the ice had retreated 65 mi (105 km)—the most rapid glacial retreat ever recorded. To preserve its clues to the world's geological history, Glacier Bay was declared a national monument in 1925. It became a national park in 1980. Today several of the glaciers in the west arm are advancing again, but very slowly.

Competition for entry permits into Glacier Bay is fierce among cruise ships. To protect the humpback whale, which feeds here in summer, the Park Service limits the number of ships that can call. Check your cruise brochure to make sure that Glacier Bay is included in your sailing. Most ships that do visit spend at least one full day exploring the park. There are no shore excursions or landings in the bay, but a Park Service naturalist boards every cruise ship to provide narration on its history and scientific importance. It is often misty or rainy, so rain gear is essential. The average summer temperature is 50° F. As always in Alaska, be prepared for the cold. Also, be sure to bring binoculars, extra film, and a telephoto lens.

The glaciers that most cruise passengers see are in the west arm of Glacier Bay. Ships linger in front of five glaciers so passengers can admire their stunning faces. Most ships stop briefly at **Reid Glacier** before continuing on to **Lamplugh Glacier**—one of the bluest in the park—at the mouth of Johns Hopkins Inlet. Next is **Johns Hopkins Glacier** at the end of the inlet, where cruise passengers are likely to see a continuous shower of calving ice. Sometimes there are

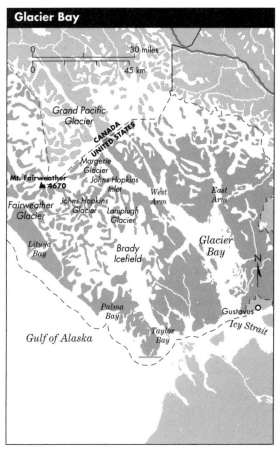

Glacier Bay

so many icebergs in the inlet that ships must avoid the area. Moving farther north, to the end of the western arm, **Margerie Glacier** is also quite active. Adjacent is **Grand Pacific Glacier,** the largest glacier in the park.

Your experience in Glacier Bay will depend partly on the size of your ship. Ocean liners tend to stay midchannel, while small yachtlike ships spend more time closer to shore. Passengers on smaller ships may get a better view of the calving ice and wildlife—such as brown and black bears, mountain goats, moose, and seals with their pups—but big-ship passengers, on vessels with much higher decks, get a loftier perspective. Both types of vessels come within ¼ mi (½ km) of the glaciers themselves.

Haines

Unlike most other cities in Southeast Alaska, Haines can be reached by road; the 152-mi (245-km) Haines Highway connects at Haines Junction with the Alaska Highway. Missionary S. Hall Young and famed naturalist John Muir picked the site for this town in 1879 as a place to bring Christianity and education to the Native populace. They could hardly have picked a more beautiful spot. The town sits on a heavily wooded peninsula with magnificent views of Portage Cove and the Coastal Mountain Range. It lies 80 mi (129 km) north of Juneau by way of fjordlike Lynn Canal.

The town has two distinct personalities. On the north side of the Haines Highway is the section of Haines founded by Young and Muir. After its missionary beginnings the town served as the trailhead for the Jack Dalton Trail to the Yukon during the 1897 Gold Rush to the Klondike. The following year, when gold was discovered in nearby Porcupine (now deserted), the booming community served as a supply center and jumping-off place for those goldfields as well. Today things are quieter; the town's streets are orderly, its homes are well kept, and for the most part it looks a great deal like any other Alaska seacoast community.

South of the highway, the town looks like a military post, which is what it was for nearly half a century. In 1903 the U.S. Army established a post—Ft. William Henry Seward— at Portage Cove just south of town. For 17 years (1922–

39) the post (renamed Chilkoot Barracks to avoid confusion with the city of Seward, farther north in the south central part of the state) was the only military base in the territory. That changed with World War II, when the army built both the Alaska Highway and the Haines Highway to link Alaska with the other states.

After the war the post closed down, and a group of veterans purchased the property from the government. They changed its name to Port Chilkoot and created residences, businesses, and a Native American arts center from the officers' houses and military buildings that surrounded the old fort's parade ground. Eventually Port Chilkoot merged with the city of Haines. Although the two areas are now officially one municipality, the old military post with its grassy parade ground is referred to as Ft. Seward.

The Haines–Ft. Seward community today is recognized for the Native American dance and culture center at Ft. Seward, as well as for the superb fishing, camping, and outdoor recreation at Chilkoot Lake, Portage Cove, Mosquito Lake, and Chilkat State Park on the shores of Chilkat Inlet. The last locale, one of the small treasures of the Alaska state park system, features views of the Davidson and Rainbow glaciers across the water.

Several of the larger ships come to Haines in the evening after spending the day in nearby Skagway, allowing passengers to enjoy salmon bakes and Chilkat Indian dancing.

Coming Ashore
Cruise ships dock in front of Ft. Seward, and downtown Haines is just a short walk away (about ⅔ mi/1 km). You can pick up walking-tour maps of both Haines and Ft. Seward at the visitor center on 2nd Avenue (tel. 907/766–2234 or 800/458–3579). Most cruise lines provide a complimentary shuttle service to downtown. Taxis are always standing by; hour-long taxi tours of the town cost $10 per person. A one-way trip between the pier and town costs $5. If you need to call for a pickup, contact **Haines Taxi** (tel. 907/766–3138) or **The Other Guys Taxi** (tel. 907/766– 3257).

Exploring Haines
Numbers in the margin correspond to points of interest on the Haines map.

❶ The **Sheldon Museum and Cultural Center,** near the foot of Main Street, houses Native artifacts—including famed Chilkat blankets—plus gold-rush memorabilia such as Jack Dalton's sawed-off shotgun. *11 Main St., tel. 907/766-2366. Admission: $3. Open daily 1–5 and whenever cruise ships are in port.*

❷ The building that houses the **Chilkat Center for the Arts** was once Ft. Seward's recreation hall, but now it features Chilkat Indian dancing. Some performances may be at the tribal house next door; check posted notices for performance times. *Ft. Seward, tel. 907/766-2160. Admission: $10. Performances Sun.–Thurs. evenings.*

❸ At **Alaska Indian Arts,** a nonprofit organization dedicated to the revival of Tlingit art forms, you'll see Native carvers making totems, metalsmiths working in silver, and weavers making blankets. *Between Chilkat Center for the Arts and Haines parade ground, tel. 907/766-2160. $1 donation requested. Open weekdays 9–noon and 1–5, and whenever cruise ships are in port.*

Celebrating Haines's location in the "Valley of the Eagles"
❹ is the **American Bald Eagle Foundation.** Inside this small museum is a diorama with stuffed local animals, but the primary focus here is bald eagles. Visitors learn about these majestic birds and the nearby Chilkat Bald Eagle Preserve just north of town (*see* Chapter 3) through lectures, displays, and videos. A gift shop sells natural history items. *2nd Ave. and Haines Hwy., tel. 907/766-3094. Admission $2. Open weekdays 9–6, weekends 1–4.*

Sports
HIKING

Battery Point Trail is a fairly level path that hugs the shoreline for two and a half miles, providing fine views across Lynn Canal. The trail begins at Portage Cove Campground (a mile east of Haines). For other hikes, pick up a copy of "Haines Is for Hikers" at the visitor center (*see* Coming Ashore, *above*).

Dining
$–$$ **Chilkat Restaurant and Bakery.** Family-style cooking is served in a homelike, no-smoking setting with lace curtains. Seafood, steaks, and sandwiches are cooked to order; Fri-

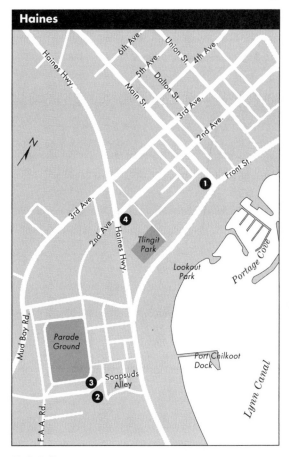

Haines

Alaska Indian
Arts, **3**

American
Bald Eagle
Foundation, **4**

Chilkat Center
for the Arts, **2**

Sheldon
Museum and
Cultural
Center, **1**

day is all-you-can-eat Mexican night. The bakery has tasty pastries to go. *5th Ave. near Main St., tel. 907/766–2920. AE, MC, V. Closed Sun.*

$–$$ Commander's Room. Stop here for fresh seafood, fish-and-chips, burgers, and more. Facing Ft. Seward's parade ground, this restaurant in Hotel Halsingland is a good place to soak up atmosphere. *At Ft. Seward, tel. 907/766–2000 or 800/542–6363. AE, DC, MC, V.*

$–$$ Lighthouse Restaurant. You get a great view of Lynn Canal from this restaurant at the foot of Main Street next to the boat harbor. Steaks, seafood, and barbecued ribs are the standards here. Save room for a slice of their famous buttermilk pie. *Front St. on the harbor, tel. 907/766–2442. AE, MC, V.*

$ Mountain Market & Deli. This spot is a bit out of the way, but it's a great place to have a mocha or latte and get in synch with Haines's outdoorsy-artist crowd. The fare includes fresh baked goods, soups, and sandwiches. *3rd Ave. at Haines Hwy., tel. 907/766–3340. MC, V.*

Saloons

Commercial fisherfolk gather nightly at the circa 1907 **Harbor Bar** (Front St. at the Harbor, tel. 907/766–2444) next to the Lighthouse Restaurant. Sometimes there's live music. It's colorful but can get a little loud at night.

Homer

Of the hundreds of thousands of cruise passengers who visit Alaska each year, only a very few get to see Homer. It's a shame. In a state of beautiful places, Homer's scenic setting on Kachemak Bay, surrounded by mountains, spruce forest, and glaciers, has attracted a sizable artists' colony. Those travelers who do arrive by ship are usually beginning or ending an expedition cruise to the Arctic or traveling aboard an Alaska Marine Highway ferry (*see* Chapter 4). Fortunately, Homer is easily reached from Seward, where all Gulf of Alaska cruises start or finish. If you rent a car, Homer is just 173 mi (279 km) down the Sterling Highway—practically next door by Alaskan standards. Direct bus connections are also available from both Anchorage and Seward; contact **Homer Stage** (tel. 907/235–2252).

The city of Homer lies at the base of a long sandy spit that juts into Kachemak Bay. It was founded just before the turn of the century as a gold-prospecting camp and later became a coal-mining headquarters. Today the town is a funky fishing port with picturesque buildings, good seafood, and beautiful bay views. It's a favorite weekend spot for Anchorage residents needing a change of scene and weather. Halibut fishing is especially good in this area.

Coming Ashore

Cruise ships dock at the Homer Spit. Fishing charters, restaurants, and shops line the spit, or passengers can take a taxi to town, where local galleries and additional dining are found. For door-to-door service, call **Chuck's Cab** (tel. 907/235–2489). A ride from the spit into town will set you back $10-$12 one-way for the first person and $1 for each additional passenger. You can also ride the **Homer Trolley** (907/235–8624), which runs every hour from 10 AM to 6 PM between the spit and downtown. The fare is $5 for adults.

Exploring Homer

For an introduction to Homer's history, visit the **Pratt Museum,** which offers three saltwater aquariums and exhibits on pioneers, Native Americans, and the 1989 Prince William Sound oil spill. Outside is a wildflower garden and a ⅓-mi (½-km) nature trail. The museum also leads 1½-hour walking tours of the harbor for $10 per person. *Bartlett St., just off Pioneer Ave., tel. 907/235–8635. Admission: $5. Open daily 10–6.*

Kachemak Bay abounds in wildlife. Shore excursions or local tour operators take visitors to bird rookeries in the bay or across the bay to gravel beaches for clam digging. Many Homer visitors come to fish for salmon or halibut. Most fishing charters include an opportunity to view whales, seals, sea otters, porpoises, and seabirds close-up. Walking along the docks on Homer Spit at the end of the day you can watch commercial fishing boats and charter boats unload their catch. The bay supports a large population of puffins and eagles.

Directly across Kachemak Bay from the end of the Homer Spit, **Halibut Cove** is a small community of people who make their living on the bay or by selling handicrafts. The Cen-

tral Charter (tel. 907/235–7847 or 800/478–7847) booking agency runs frequent boats to the cove from Homer.
Halibut Cove has an art gallery and a restaurant that serves
local seafood. The cove itself is lovely, especially during
salmon runs, when fish leap and splash in the clear water.
There are also several lodges on this side of the bay, on pristine coves away from summer crowds.

Seldovia, isolated across the bay from Homer, retains the
charm of an earlier Alaska. The town's Russian heritage is
evident in its onion-dome church and its name, derived from
a Russian place-name meaning "herring bay." Those who
fish use plenty of herring for bait, catching salmon, halibut,
and king or Dungeness crab. You'll find excellent fishing
whether you drop your line into the deep waters of
Kachemak Bay or cast into the surf for silver salmon on
the shore of Outside Beach, near town. Self-guided hiking
or berry picking in late July are other options. Seldovia can
be reached from Homer by boat, and the dock of the small
boat harbor is in the center of town—allowing for easy exploration. For a guided historical tour, contact South Shore
Tours (tel. 907/234–8000).

Shopping
The galleries on and around Pioneer Avenue are good
places to find works by the town's residents. For contemporary art pieces, head to **Bunnell Street Galley** (106 W. Bunnell St., tel. 907/235– 2662)—it's next to the Two Sisters
coffeehouse (*see below*).

Dining
$$$ Homestead Restaurant. Eight miles (13 kilometers) from
town, this log roadhouse overlooking Kachemak Bay is
where locals take guests for a night out. The fare here in-
cludes Caesar salads, steak, prime rib, and fresh seafood;
the flavors are rich with spicy ethnic sauces. *Mile 8.2 East
End Rd., tel. 907/235–8723. AE, MC, V.*

$$$ The Saltry in Halibut Cove. Exotically prepared local seafood
dishes, including curries and pastas, and a wide selection
of imported beers are served here. The deck overlooks the
boat dock and the cove. It's a good place to while away
the afternoon or evening, meandering along the boardwalk, visiting galleries, and finishing with a meal here.
Take the Danny J *ferry ($21 round- trip) from Homer har-*

bor; tel. 907/235–7847. *Reservations essential. MC, V. Open summer only.*

$ Café Cups. With microbrewery beer on tap and local artists' works on the walls, this renovated house offers more than just great food, fresh-baked breads, and desserts. Locals and visitors alike crowd into the cozy dining room for coffee and conversation in the morning or later in the day for fresh pasta, local seafood, and an eclectic but reasonably priced wine selection. Desserts include a triple-decadent cheesecake and black-bottom almond cream pie. The outside deck is a fine place to enjoy a lazy morning while savoring your eggs Florentine. *162 W. Pioneer Ave., tel. 907/235–8330. AE, MC, V.*

$ Two Sisters. For a delightful taste of the real Homer, visit this tiny coffeehouse-bakery housed in a historic building. The funky, mixed crowd here includes fisherfolk, writers, and local businesspeople drinking perfectly brewed espresso, talking politics, and sampling pastries that are to die for. Two Sisters gets crowded on weekend mornings—you'll see folks overflowing onto the porch. *106 W. Bunnell St., tel. 907/235–2280. No credit cards.*

Saloon

The **Salty Dawg Saloon** (tel. 907/235–9990) is famous all over Alaska. Fisherfolk, cannery workers, and carpenters have been holding court for decades in this friendly and noisy pub. Today they're joined by college kids working in the gift shops, retirees, and tourists. Near the end of the spit, the Salty Dawg is easy to find; just look for the "lighthouse."

Tastes of Alaska

Alaska Wild Berry Products (528 Pioneer Ave., tel. 907/235–8858 or 800/280–2927) manufactures jams, jellies, sauces, syrups, and chocolate-covered candies made from wild berries handpicked on the Kenai Peninsula and a large selection of Alaska-theme gifts and clothing; shipping is available.

Juneau

Juneau owes its origins to a trio of colorful characters: two pioneers, Joe Juneau and Dick Harris, and a Tlingit chief named Kowee, who discovered rich reserves of gold in the stream that now runs through the middle of town. That was in 1880, and shortly after the discovery a modest stampede led first to the establishment of a camp, then a town, then the Alaska territorial (now state) capital.

For nearly 60 years after Juneau's founding, gold remained the mainstay of the economy. In its heyday, the Alaska Juneau gold mine was the biggest low-grade-ore mine in the world. Then, during World War II, the government decided it needed Juneau's manpower for the war effort, and the mines ceased operations. After the war, mining failed to start up again, and the government became the city's principal employer.

Juneau is a charming, cosmopolitan frontier town. It's easy to navigate, has one of the best museums in Alaska, is surrounded by beautiful (and accessible) wilderness, and has a glacier in its backyard. To capture the true frontier ambience, stop by the Red Dog Saloon or the Alaskan Hotel. Both are on the main shopping drag, just a quick walk from the cruise-ship pier.

Coming Ashore

Most cruise ships dock or tender passengers ashore at **Marine Park** or at the old **Ferry Terminal.** Princess ships (and some others) tie up at the **South Franklin Dock.** Ask aboard your ship exactly which facility you'll be using. Both Marine Park and the Ferry Terminal are within easy walking distance of the downtown shops and attractions. The South Franklin Dock is about a fifth of a mile, or an eight-minute walk, from the edge of downtown and the new Mt. Roberts tram. For those who prefer not to walk, a shuttle bus ($1 round-trip) runs from the dock to town whenever ships are in town.

For visitor information, there's a small kiosk filled with tour brochures, bus schedules, and maps on the pier at Marine Park; it is staffed when ships are in port. There is a tourist information center at the old ferry terminal as well. The downtown shops along South Franklin Street are just minutes away.

You won't need to hire a taxi in Juneau unless you are heading to Mendenhall Glacier. In that case, taxis will be waiting for you at Marine Park. Another option is the city bus that stops on South Franklin Street. For $1.25, it'll take you within 1¼ mi (2 km) of the Mendenhall Visitor Center. The **Glacier Express** (tel. 907/789–0052 or 800/478–0052) provides direct bus service between downtown and the glacier for $10 round-trip.

Exploring Juneau

Numbers in the margin correspond to points of interest on the Juneau map.

❶ A block east of the cruise ship docks at Marine Park is **South Franklin Street.** The buildings here and on Front Street, which intersects South Franklin several blocks north, are among the oldest and most interesting in the city. Many reflect the architecture of the 1920s and '30s; some are even older.

At No. 278 South Franklin Street is the **Red Dog Saloon.** With a sawdust-covered floor, a stuffed bear, and big-game heads mounted on the walls, this is Alaska's most famous saloon.

Just down the street from the Red Dog is the small **Alaskan Hotel** (167 S. Franklin St.), which was called "a pocket edition of the best hotels on the Pacific Coast" when it opened in 1913. The building has been lovingly restored with period trappings. The barroom's massive, mirrored oak bar, accented by Tiffany lamps and panels, is a particular delight.

Also on South Franklin Street is the **Alaska Steam Laundry Building,** a 1901 structure with a windowed turret. It now houses a great collection of photos from Juneau's past, a popular espresso shop (Heritage Coffee Co., tel. 907/586–1752), and several stores.

Across the street from the Steam Laundry Building, the equally venerable **Senate Building Mall** (175 S. Franklin St.) contains a fine gallery with Native arts and jewelry, a place to buy Russian icons, and even a shop selling goods from Ireland.

❷ At the corner of Seward Street is the **Alaska State Capitol,** constructed in 1930, with pillars of southeastern-Alaska marble. The structure now houses the governor's office and other state agencies, and the state legislature meets here from January through May each year. *Tel. 907/465–2479. Tours weekdays 9–4:30 in summer.*

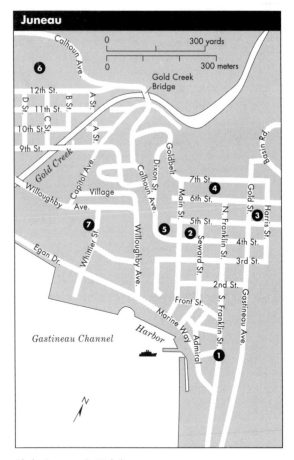

Juneau

| 0 | | 300 yards |
| 0 | | 300 meters |

Gold Creek Bridge

Calhoun Ave.

12th St.
11th St.
10th St.
9th St.

D St.
B St.
C St.
A St.

Gold Creek

Willoughby

A St.

Goldbelt

Dixon St.

Main St.

Calhoun Ave.

Capitol Ave.

Village Ave.

Willoughby Ave.

Whittier St.

Egan Dr.

7th St.
6th St.
5th St.
4th St.
3rd St.
2nd St.

Seward St.

N. Franklin St.

Gold St.

Harris St.

Basin Rd.

Front St.

Marine Way

Harbor

S. Franklin St.

Admiral

Gastineau Ave.

Gastineau Channel

6
4
3
5
2
7
1

N

Alaska State
Capitol, **2**

Alaska State
Museum, **7**

Evergreen
Cemetery, **6**

House of
Wickersham, **4**

Juneau-
Douglas City
Museum, **5**

St. Nicholas
Russian
Orthodox
Church, **3**

South Franklin
Street, **1**

❸ At the top of the hill on 5th Street is little **St. Nicholas Russian Orthodox Church,** built in 1894. This is the oldest Russian church building in Southeast Alaska. Here you can see icons that date from the 1700s. *326 5th St., off Gold St., tel. 907/586–1023. Admission: $1 donation requested. Open daily for tours 9–6 in summer.*

❹ The **House of Wickersham,** the 1899 residence of James Wickersham, a pioneer judge and delegate to Congress, houses memorabilia from the judge's travels, ranging from rare Native American basketry and ivory carvings to historic photos, 47 diaries, and a Chickering grand piano that came "round the horn" to Alaska when the Russians still ruled the region. The tour includes full narration by costumed guides and tea and sourdough bread with "the judge." *213 7th St., tel. 907/586–9001. Admission and complete tour: $7.50. Open Tues.–Sun. 10–3.*

❺ Two fine totem poles flank the entrance to the **Juneau-Douglas City Museum.** Inside, the city's history is relayed through memorabilia, gold-mining exhibits, and videos. *4th and Main Sts., tel. 907/586–3572. Admission: $2. Open weekdays 9–5, weekends 10–5.*

❻ **Evergreen Cemetery** is where many Juneau pioneers (including Joe Juneau and Dick Harris) are buried. At the end of the gravel lane is the monument to Chief Kowee, who was cremated on this spot.

❼ The **Alaska State Museum** is one of Alaska's best, with exhibits on the state's history, Native cultures, wildlife, industry, and art. *395 Whittier St., tel. 907/465–2901. Admission: $4. Open weekdays 9–6, weekends 10–6.*

One of Juneau's most popular sights, **Mendenhall Glacier** is just 13 mi (21 km) from downtown. The visitor center here provides information and videos; nearby hiking trails offer magnificent views of the glacier itself. A visit to the glacier is included in most Juneau bus tours.

For a great view of the harbor, take the **Mt. Roberts Tram** (490 S. Franklin St., tel. 907/463–3412 or 888/461-8726) to an observation deck 2,000 ft above Juneau. Walking paths lead from the visitors center (*see* Hiking, *below*), which also has retail shops, a restaurant and bar, a nature center, and an auditorium that shows films on Native culture. You can catch the tram from the base terminal downtown—it's within walking distance of the cruise-ship piers. The tram and all facilities are wheelchair accessible. For $19.75 you get unlimited rides for the day.

Shopping

South Franklin Street is the place in Juneau to shop. The variety of merchandise is good, though some shops offer an abundance of Made-in-China Alaskan keepsakes. You'll pay high prices for authentic Native handicrafts or hand-knitted sweaters. One of the better galleries is **Mt. Juneau Artists** (211 Front St., tel. 907/586–2108), an arts and crafts cooperative.

In the Senate Building Mall on South Franklin Street is the **Russian Shop** (tel. 907/586–2778), a repository of icons, samovars, lacquered boxes, nesting dolls, and other items that reflect Alaska's 18th- and 19th-century Russian heritage.

For a souvenir from one of Alaska's most famous saloons, stop by the gift shop at the **Red Dog Saloon** (*see* Exploring Juneau, *above*).

Prints from one of Alaska's best-known artists, Rie Muñoz, are sold at **Decker Gallery** (233 S. Franklin St., tel. 907/463–5536 or 800/463–5536). Her bright works use stylized designs, bright swirls of colors, and often feature Native Alaskans. Another fun place to browse is the **Wm. Spear Designs Gallery** (165 S. Franklin St., tel. 907/586–2209). His colorful enameled pins are witty, creative, amusing, and sometimes simply perverse. Hundreds of different designs are available.

Sports

FISHING

More than 30 charter-boat operators offer fishing trips in the Juneau area; stop by the **Davis Log Cabin** (3rd and Seward Sts., tel. 907/586–2201) for a complete listing.

HIKING

Surrounded by the **Tongass National Forest,** Juneau is a hiker's paradise. For trail maps, information, and advice, stop by Centennial Hall on Willoughby at Egan Drive (tel. 907/586–8751).

The **Davis Log Cabin** (3rd and Seward Sts., tel. 907/586–2201) sells two useful booklets: "90 Short Walks Around Juneau" ($5) and "Juneau Trails" ($4). Good trails for cruise passengers begin just behind the **Mendenhall Glacier Visitor Center** (*see* Exploring Juneau, *above*).

The **Juneau Parks and Recreation Department** (tel. 907/586–5226) sponsors Wednesday-morning and Saturday group hikes. On Saturday, there's free car-pool pickup at the docks.

Gastineau Guiding (tel. 907/586–2666) leads guided hikes in the Juneau area. A 2-hour tour starts at the dock and features a city tour, a Mt. Roberts tram ride, and a 1-hour alpine hike for $40. They also offer a 3-hour rain-forest nature tour and walk on Douglas Island for $60.

KAYAKING

Auk Ta Shaa Discovery (tel. 907/586–8687 or 800/820–2628) leads raft and kayak trips down the Mendenhall River, plus all-day sea kayaking adventures ($95 per person). Lunch and rain gear are included. Trips leave around 9:30 AM and return about 4 PM, so participation is practical only for passengers whose ships make day-long calls.

Dining

$–$$$ **Fiddlehead Restaurant and Bakery.** Definitely a favorite with Juneau locals, this delightful place decorated with light wood, stained glass, and historic photos serves generous portions of healthy fare. How about a light meal of black beans and rice? Or pasta Greta Garbo (locally smoked salmon tossed with fettuccine in cream sauce). Their bakery always has delicious breads, croissants, and sweets. Upstairs, the Fireweed Room features a more diverse menu, along with folk and jazz music most nights. *429 W. Willoughby Ave., tel. 907/586–3150. AE, D, DC, MC, V.*

$$ **Hanger on the Wharf.** Popular with both locals and travelers, this casual dining place has expansive views of Gastineau Channel and Douglas Island. A wide selection of entrées, including locally caught halibut and salmon, filet mignon, and prawn linguini, makes this a Juneau hot spot. Upstairs are pool tables and a dance club with live music on weekends. *2 Marine Way, tel. 907/586–5018. AE, D, MC, V.*

$ Armadillo Tex-Mex Cafe. A devoted clientele of locals waits in line to order border eats at this bustling, boisterous café. Check the daily specials, or if you aren't too hungry order a big bowl of homemade chili and cornbread. *431 S. Franklin St., tel. 907/586–1880. MC, V.*

Saloons

Juneau is one of the best saloon towns in all of Alaska. Try stopping in one of the following:

The **Red Dog Saloon** (278 S. Franklin St., tel. 907/463–3777) carries on the sawdust-on-the-floor tradition, with a mounted bear and other game trophies on the walls and lots of historic photos. There's live music and the crowd is raucous, especially when cruise ships are in port.

The **Alaskan Hotel Bar** (167 S. Franklin St., tel. 907/586–1000) is popular with locals and distinctly less touristy. If live music isn't playing, an old-fashioned player piano usually is.

The comfortable **Bubble Room** (127 N. Franklin St., tel. 907/586–2660) lounge off the lobby in the Baranof Hotel is quiet—and sees (so it is said) more legislative lobbying and decision making than the nearby state capitol building. The music from the piano bar is soft.

Tastes of Alaska

When you're "shopping" the bars and watering holes of Southeast Alaska, ask for Alaskan Amber, Frontier Beer, or Pale Ale. All are brewed and bottled in Juneau. If you'd like to see how these award-winning brews are crafted, visit the **Alaskan Brewing Company.** *5429 Shaune Dr., tel. 907/780–5866. Open Mon.– Sat. 11–4:30.*

At **Taku Smokeries** (550 S. Franklin St., tel. 800/582–5122), on the south end of town near the cruise-ship docks, you can view the smoking process through large windows and then purchase packaged fish in the deli-style gift shop. They can also ship fish home for you.

Kenai Peninsula

Salmon and halibut fishing, scenery, and wildlife are the standouts of the Kenai Peninsula, which thrusts into the Gulf of Alaska south of Anchorage. Commercial fishing is im-

Finally, a travel companion that doesn't snore on the plane or eat all your peanuts.

When traveling, your MCI WorldCom Card is the best way to keep in touch. Our operators speak your language, so they'll be able to connect you back home—no matter where your travels take you. Plus, your MCI WorldCom Card is easy to use, and even earns you frequent flyer miles every time you use it. When you add in our great rates, you get something even more valuable: peace-of-mind. So go ahead. Travel the world. MCI WorldCom just brought it a whole lot closer.

You can even sign up today at www.mci.com/worldphone or ask your operator to make a collect call to 1-410-314-2938.

EASY TO CALL WORLDWIDE

1 Just dial the WorldPhone access number of the country you're calling from.
2 Dial or give the operator your MCI WorldCom Card number.
3 Dial or give the number you're calling.

Aruba	**800-888-8**
Bahamas/Bermuda	**1-800-888-8000**
British Virgin Islands	**1-800-888-8000**
China	
Available from most major cities	**108-12**
For a Mandarin-speaking Operator	**108-17**
Costa Rica ◆	**0-800-012-2222**
Japan ◆	
To call using JT	**0044-11-121**
To call using KDD	**00539-121▶**
To call using IDC	**0066-55-121**

For your complete WorldPhone calling guide, dial the WorldPhone access number for the country you're in and ask the operator for Customer Service. In the U.S. call 1-800-431-5402.

◆ Public phones may require deposit of coin or phone card for dial tone.
▶ Regulation does not permit Intra-Japan calls.

EARN FREQUENT FLYER MILES

American Airlines
A'Advantage®

Continental Airlines
OnePass

▲ Delta Air Lines
SkyMiles®

✈ MILEAGE PLUS®
United Airlines

U·S AIRWAYS
DIVIDEND MILES

MCI WorldCom, its logo and the names of the products referred to herein are proprietary marks of MCI WorldCom, Inc. All airline names and logos are proprietary marks of the respective airlines. All airline program rules and conditions apply.

Don't Forget To Pack A Nikon.

PRONEA *S*

The technology of a serious camera.
The spontaneity of a point-and-shoot.

The Nikon Pronea S, the world's smallest and lightest SLR, is the easiest way to bring memories of your next vacation home with you. Serious camera technology. Three picture formats. Interchangeable zoom lenses. Point-and-shoot simplicity. At 15 ounces, it's ready to go anywhere you go. For more information, visit us at *www.nikonusa.com*

Nikon

PRONEA *S*

portant to the area's economy, and the city of Kenai, on the peninsula's northwest coast, is the base for the Cook Inlet offshore oil fields.

The area is dotted with roadside campgrounds, and you can explore three major federal holdings on the peninsula—the western end of the sprawling **Chugach National Forest,** along with **Kenai National Wildlife Refuge** and **Kenai Fjords National Park.**

Portage Glacier, 50 mi (80 km) southeast of Anchorage, is one of Alaska's most heavily visited tourist destinations. A 6-mi (10-km) side road off the Seward Highway leads to the Begich-Boggs Visitor Center (tel. 907/783–2326) on the shore of Portage Lake. The center houses impressive displays on glaciers. Boat tours of the face of the glacier are conducted aboard the 200-passenger *Ptarmigan.* Unfortunately, the glacier is rapidly receding and is no longer pushing so many icebergs into the lake, so the views are not what they once were.

The mountains surrounding Portage Glacier are covered with smaller glaciers. A short hike to Byron Glacier Overlook, about a mile (1½ km) west, is popular in the spring and summer. Twice weekly in summer, naturalists lead free treks in search of microscopic ice worms. Keep an eye out for black bears in all the Portage side valleys in the summer.

Ketchikan

Situated at the base of 3,000-ft Deer Mountain, Ketchikan is the definitive Southeast Alaska town. Houses cling to the steep hillsides and the harbors are filled with fishing boats. Until miners and fishermen settled here in the 1880s, the mouth of Ketchikan Creek was a summer fishing camp for the Tlingit people. Today the town runs on fishing, tourism, logging, and government.

Ketchikan is Alaska's totem-pole port: at the nearby Tlingit village of Saxman, 2½ mi (4 km) south of downtown, there is a major totem park, and residents still practice traditional carving techniques. The Ketchikan Visitors Bureau on the dock can supply information on getting to Saxman on your own, or you can take a ship-organized tour.

Another excellent outdoor totem display is at Totem Bight State Historical Park, a coastal rain forest 10 mi (16 km) north of town. The Totem Heritage Center preserves historic poles, some nearly 200 years old.

Expect rain at some time during the day, even if the sun is shining when you dock: the average annual precipitation is more than 150 inches.

Coming Ashore

Ships dock or tender passengers ashore directly across from the **Ketchikan Visitors Bureau** (tel. 907/225–6166 or 800/770–3300) on Front and Mission streets, in the center of downtown. Here you can pick up brochures and maps.

The impressive **Southeast Alaska Visitor Center** has exhibits on Native culture, wildlife, logging, recreation, and the use of public lands. You can also watch its award-winning film "Mystical Southeast Alaska." *50 Main St., tel. 907/228–6214. Admission: $4. Open daily 8:30–4:30.*

Ketchikan is easy to explore, with walking-tour signs to lead you around the city. Most of the town's sights are within easy walking distance. A new paved bike-and-walking path leads to the city of Saxman for those who wish to visit the Native village—but remember it's 2½ mi (4 km) from downtown Ketchikan.

To reach the sights outside downtown on your own, you'll want to hire a cab or ride the local buses. Metered taxis meet the ships right on the docks and also wait across the street. Rates are $2.10 for pickup, 23¢ each ⅒ mi.

Exploring Ketchikan

Numbers in the margin correspond to points of interest on the Ketchikan map.

 You can learn about Ketchikan's early days of fishing, mining, and logging at the **Tongass Historical Museum.** *In the library building at Dock and Bawden Sts., tel. 907/225–5600. Admission: $3. Open daily 8–5 in summer.*

For a great view of the harbor, take curving Venetia Avenue to the **Westmark Cape Fox Lodge.** Not only are the views stunning but the dining is excellent. You can also take a tramway ride ($1) up the hillside from popular Creek Street (*see below*).

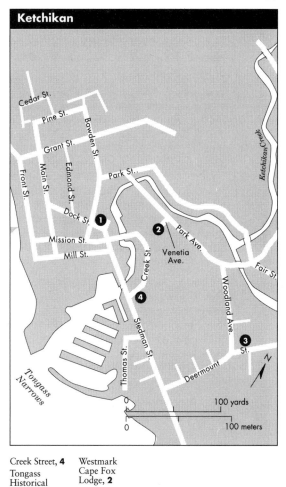

Ketchikan

Creek Street, **4**

Tongass
Historical
Museum, **1**

Totem
Heritage
Center, **3**

Westmark
Cape Fox
Lodge, **2**

❸ Every visitor to Ketchikan should stop by the **Totem Heritage Center,** which has a fascinating display of weathered, original totem carvings. *Woodland Ave. at corner of Deermont St., tel. 907/225–5900. Admission: $4. Open daily 8–5 in summer.*

❹ **Creek Street,** formerly Ketchikan's infamous red-light district, remains the picturesque centerpiece of town. Its small houses, built on stilts over the creek, have been restored as trendy shops. The street's most famous brothel, **Dolly's House** (tel. 907/225–6329; admission: $4), has been preserved as a museum, complete with original furnishings and a short history of the life and times of Ketchikan's best-known madam. There's good salmon viewing in season at the Creek Street footbridge. You can catch the tram here for a ride up to the Westmark Cape Fox Lodge, if you missed it before (*see above*).

Shopping

Because artists are local, prices for Native American crafts are better in Ketchikan than at most other ports. The **Saxman Village** gift shop has some Tlingit wares along with less expensive mass-produced souvenirs. A better bet is to head a block downhill to **Saxman Arts Co-op** (tel. 907/225–4166) where the baskets, button blankets (traditional wool blankets, usually bright red, with designs made from ivory-colored buttons sewn into the fabric), moccasins, wood carvings, and jewelry are all locally made.

Creek Street has several attractive boutiques. At **Parnassus Bookstore** (5 Creek St., tel. 907/225–7690), you can browse through an eclectic collection of books. The same building houses two fine-arts and crafts shops: **Alaska Eagle Arts** (tel. 907/225– 8365) and **Soho Coho** (tel. 907/225–5954). The latter is the headquarters for artist Ray Troll, Alaska's famed producer of all things weird and fishy.

Salmon, Etc. (322 Mission St., tel. 907/225–6008) sells every form of Alaskan salmon, which can be sent, frozen and processed, to your home.

Sports

FISHING

Salmon are so plentiful in these waters that the town has earned the nickname "Salmon Capital of the World." Contact the **Ketchikan Convention & Visitors Bureau** (131 Front St., 99901, tel. 907/225–6166 or 800/770–2200) for a full list of charter companies; they will send you a vacation planner as well.

HIKING

Check at the visitors bureau on the dock for trail maps and advice. If you're a tough hiker with sturdy shoes, the trail from downtown (starting at the end of Fair Street) to the top of 3,000-ft **Deer Mountain** will repay your effort with a spectacular panorama of the city below and the wilderness behind. It's 6 mi (10 km) round-trip. The **Ward Lake Area,** about 6 mi (10 km) north of town, offers easier hiking along lakes and streams and beneath towering spruce and hemlock trees.

The Southeast Alaska Visitor Center (*see* Coming Ashore, *above*) has trail maps detailing these and other U.S. Forest Service trails.

KAYAKING AND CANOEING

Both **Southeast Exposure** (507 Stedman St., tel. 907/225–8829) and **Southeast Sea Kayaks** (tel. 907/225–1258) offer sea-kayak rentals, instruction, and tours. Three-hour tours (all gear included) cost around $70.

Dining

$$–$$$ **Annabelle's Keg and Chowder House.** In the Gilmore Hotel, this seafood restaurant takes you back to the 1920s. The walls are covered with photos and paintings depicting the Ketchikan of years past. Specials include clams, oysters on the half shell, delicious seafood chowders, prime rib, and pasta. Afterward, be sure to order a slice of peanut-butter pie. There's also an espresso bar and Annabelle's, a semi-formal lounge with a jukebox. *326 Front St., tel. 907/ 225–6009. AE, D, DC, MC, V.*

$$–$$$ **Steamers.** This spacious restaurant sits right next to the dock in the new Spruce Mill Mall. Menu specials include seafood of all types, and the bar claims to have more beer taps than any other Southeast Alaska establishment. *76 Front St., tel. 907/225–1600. AE, D, DC, MC, V.*

Saloons

Annabelle's Keg and Chowder House (326 Front St., tel. 907/225– 6009), a restaurant-lounge with a jukebox in the

Gilmore Hotel, blends old and new Alaska in a semiformal atmosphere. There's no pretense of formality at the **Potlatch Bar** (tel. 907/225–4855) in Thomas Basin, where local fisherfolk and cannery workers play pool and tip back cans of Rainier Beer.

For a bright and spacious no-smoking bar with a dozen microbrews on tap, head to **Kingfisher Bar** (tel. 907/247–5227), upstairs in the Salmon Landing Mall at the corner of Mill and Front streets. Big windows face the cruise-ship dock and Tongass Narrows, and you can listen to live bands on weekends.

Misty Fjords National Monument

In the past, cruise ships used to bypass Misty Fjords on their way up and down the Inside Passage. But today more and more cruise passengers are discovering its unspoiled beauty. Ships big and small, from the yachtlike vessels of Alaska Sightseeing to the liners of Crystal, Cunard, Norwegian Cruise Line, and others, now feature a day of scenic cruising through this protected wilderness. At the southern end of the Inside Passage, Misty Fjords usually lies just before or after a call at Ketchikan. The attraction here is the wilderness—3,500 square mi of it—highlighted by waterfalls and cliffs that rise 3,000 ft. If your ship doesn't visit Misty, consider taking a tour of the area from **Alaska Cruises** (tel. 907/225–6044 or 800/228–1905) when you visit nearby Ketchikan.

Petersburg

Getting to Petersburg is an experience. Only ferries and the smallest cruise ships can squeak through Wrangell Narrows, with the aid of more than 50 buoys and markers along the 22-mi (35-km) crossing. At times the channel seems too narrow for ships to pass through, making for a nail-biting—though safe—trip. The inaccessibility of Petersburg is part of its off-the-beaten-path charm. Unlike several other Southeast communities, this one never overwhelms with hordes of cruise-ship passengers.

At your first glimpse of Petersburg you may think you're in the old country. Neat, white, Scandinavian-style homes and storefronts with steep roofs and decorated with bright-colored swirls of leaf-and-flower designs (called rosemaling) and row upon row of sturdy fishing vessels in the harbor invoke the spirit of Norway. No wonder. This prosperous fishing community was founded by Norwegian Peter Buschmann in 1897.

The Little Norway Festival is held here each year on the third full weekend in May. If you're in town during the festival, be sure to take part in one of the fish feeds that highlight the Norwegian Independence Day celebration. The beer-batter halibut is delectable, and you won't find better folk dancing outside of Norway.

Coming Ashore

Ships small enough to visit Petersburg dock in the South Harbor, which is about a ½-mi (1-km) walk to downtown. Everything in Petersburg, including the **Petersburg Visitor Information Center** on 1st and Fram streets (tel. 907/772–4636), is within easy walking distance of the harbor. Renting a bicycle is an especially pleasant way to see the sights. A good route is to ride along the coast on Nordic Drive, past the lovely homes, to the boardwalk and the city dump, where you might spot some bears. Coming back to town, take the interior route and you'll pass the airport and some pretty churches before returning to the waterfront. Bicycles are available for rent from **Northern Bikes** (110 N. Nordic Dr., tel. 907/772–3978) at the Scandia House Hotel.

Passengers who want to learn about the local history, the commercial fishing industry, and the natural history of the Tongass National Forest can book a guided van tour. Contact **See Alaska Tours and Charters** (tel. 907/772–4656).

Exploring Petersburg

Numbers in the margin correspond to points of interest on the Petersburg map.

One of the most pleasant things to do in Petersburg is to roam among the fishing vessels tied up at dockside. This is one of Alaska's busiest, most prosperous fishing communities, and the variety of boats is enormous. You'll see small trollers, big halibut vessels, and sleek pleasure craft as well. Wander, too, around the fish-processing structures (though beware of the pungent aroma). Just by watching shrimp, salmon, or halibut catches being brought ashore, you can get a real appreciation for this industry and the people who engage in it.

Overlooking the city harbor there are great vantage points. The peaks of the Coastal Range behind the town mark the border between Canada and the United States; the most striking is **Devils Thumb,** at 9,077 ft. About 25 mi (40 km) east of Petersburg lies spectacular **LeConte Glacier,** the continent's southernmost tidewater glacier and one of its most active ones. It often happens that so many icebergs have calved into the bay that the entrance is carpeted bank-to-bank with floating bergs. The glacier is accessible only by water or air.

For a scenic hike closer to town, go north on Nordic Drive ❶ to **Sandy Beach,** one of Petersburg's favorite spots for picnics and recreation and one that frequently offers good eagle viewing.

The best place to watch for America's national bird is the ❷ appropriately named **Eagle's Roost Park,** along the shore north of the Petersburg Fisheries cannery. At low tide you may see more than two dozen eagles here.

❸ A great photo opportunity lies in the center of town at **Hammer Slough,** where houses built on stilts make for a postcard-perfect picture. The large, white, barnlike structure on ❹ stilts that borders the slough is the **Sons of Norway Hall,** where locals keep the traditions and culture of the old country alive.

Those wishing to do some sightseeing in town should head ❺ northeast to the **Clausen Memorial Museum** and the bronze *Fisk* (Norwegian for "fish") sculpture at 2nd and Fram streets. The museum—not surprisingly—devotes a lot of its space to fishing and fish processing. There's an old "iron chink," used in the early days for gutting and cleaning fish, as well as displays that illustrate the workings of several types of fishing boats. On exhibit are a 126½-pound king salmon, the largest ever caught, which came out of a fish trap on Prince of Wales Island in 1939, and the world's largest chum salmon—a 36-pounder. Also here are displays of Native artifacts. *203 Fram St., tel. 907/772–3598. Admission: $2. Open Mon.–Sat. 9:30–4:30, Sun. 12:30–4:30 in summer.*

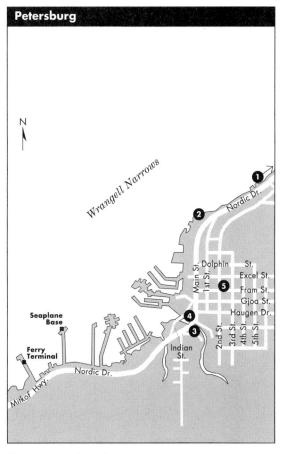

Petersburg

N

Wrangell Narrows

Nordic Dr.

Dolphin St.
Excel St.
Fram St.
Gjoa St.
Haugen Dr.

Main St.
1st St.
2nd St.
3rd St.
4th St.
5th St.

Indian St.

Nordic Dr.

Seaplane Base

Ferry Terminal

Mitkof Hwy.

Three **pioneer churches**—Catholic, Lutheran, and Presbyterian—are nearby at Dolphin and 3rd streets, Excel and 5th streets, and on Ḥaugen Street between 2nd and 3rd streets, respectively. Of the three, the 50-year-old Lutheran church is the oldest. It is said that boys would bring dirt by the wheelbarrow load for landscaping around the foundation. Their compensation? Ice-cream cones. The enticement was so successful that, after three years of ice-cream rewards, it was necessary to bring in a bulldozer to scrape off the excess dirt.

Dining

$–$$ **Pellerito's Pizza.** Although it has a few inside tables, this popular pizza joint primarily specializes in take-out pizzas, giant calzones, and hero sandwiches. You'll also find ice cream, cinnamon rolls, and espresso. *Across from ferry terminal, tel. 907/772–3727. MC, V.*

$ **Alaskafe Coffeehouse.** Looking for a smoke-free place to hang out? Alaskafe has light meals all day: panini sandwiches, homemade soups, pastas, salads, and desserts. Plus, of course, coffee. The outdoor balcony seats are nice on a sunny day, and local musicians and poets perform on Saturday evenings. *Upstairs at the corner of Nordic and Excel, tel. 907/772–5282. No credit cards.*

$ **Coastal Cold Storage Fish Market.** This is the place to go in Petersburg for fresh seafood. Although primarily a lunch eatery, they are also open for breakfast and dinner, with fish chowders, beer-batter halibut, shrimp cocktail, and sandwiches. They also ship fresh, smoked, canned, or frozen fish, or process any that you catch. *Corner of Excel and Main Sts., tel. 907/772–4171. No credit cards.*

$ **The Homestead.** There's nothing at all fancy here, just basic American fare: steaks, local prawns and halibut, a salad bar, and especially generous breakfasts. Rhubarb pie is the fastest-selling item on the menu. *217 Main St., tel. 907/772–3900. DC, MC, V.*

Saloons

The name **Harbor Bar** (Nordic Dr. near Dolphin St., tel. 907/772– 4526) suggests the decor here—ship's wheels, ship pictures, and a mounted red snapper.

A colorful, authentic Alaskan bar of regional fame, **Kito's Kave** (Sing Lee Alley, tel. 907/772–3207) serves Mexican food in a pool-hall atmosphere. It's not for the timid or faint of heart.

Tastes of Alaska

One of the Southeast's gourmet delicacies is "Petersburg shrimp." Small (they're seldom larger than half your pinky finger), tender, and succulent, they're much treasured by Alaskans, who often send them "outside" as thank-you gifts. You'll find the little critters fresh in meat departments and canned in gift sections at food stores throughout the Panhandle. You can buy fresh vacuum-packed Petersburg shrimp in Petersburg at **Coastal Cold Storage Fish Market,** downtown on Main Street, or by mail-order (tel. 907/772–4177).

Prince William Sound

Every Gulf of Alaska cruise visits Prince William Sound. The sound made worldwide headlines in 1989, when the *Exxon Valdez* hit a reef and spilled 11 million gallons of North Slope crude. The oil has sunk into the beaches below the surface, however, and vast sections of the sound appear pristine, with abundant wildlife. The lasting effects on the area of this lurking oil—sometimes uncovered after storms and high tides—is still being studied.

Numbers in the margin correspond to points of interest on the South Central Alaska map.

❶ A visit to **Columbia Glacier,** which flows from the surrounding Chugach Mountains, is included on many Gulf of Alaska cruises. Its deep aquamarine face is 5 mi (8 km) across, and it calves new icebergs with resounding cannonades. This glacier is one of the largest and most readily accessible of Alaska's coastal glaciers.

The major attraction in Prince William Sound on most ❷ Gulf of Alaska cruises is the day spent in **College Fjord.** Dubbed "Alaska's newest Glacier Bay" by one cruise line, this deep finger of water is ringed by 16 glaciers, each named after one of the colleges that sponsored early exploration of the fjord.

Of the three major Prince William Sound communities— ❸ Valdez, Whittier, and Cordova—only **Valdez** (pronounced

South Central Alaska

Denali National Park and Preserve

Denali (Mt. McKinley) ▲

Denali National Park

Healy

Cantwell

Denali

Paxson

Susitna River

ALASKA RR

Parks Hwy.

Richardson Hwy.

Petersville

Trapper Creek

Hatcher Pass Rd.

Independence Mine State Historical Park ■

Glenn Hwy.

Glennallen

Willow

Glenn

CHUGACH MTS.

Wasilla

Palmer

Sutton

Matanuska R.

Columbia Glacier ❶

Anchorage

Girdwood

College Fjord ❷

❸ **Valdez**

Tyonek

Cook Inlet

Hope

PORTAGE GLACIER

Chugach National Forest

Sterling

Kenai

Cooper Landing

Portage

Whittier

Seward Hwy.

Prince William Sound

Cordova

Clam Gulch

Soldotna

Seward

Moose Pass

Ninilchik

Sterling Hwy.

Kenai Peninsula ■

Kenai Fjords National Park

Homer

Seldovia

Anchor Point

TO KODIAK

N

KEY

- - - - Ferry Lines

——— Rail lines

0   100 miles

0   150 km

val-*deez*) is a major port of call for cruise ships. For more information on visiting Valdez, *see below.*

Seward

On the southeastern coast of the Kenai Peninsula, Seward is surrounded by four major federal landholdings—**Chugach National Forest, Kenai Wildlife Refuge, Kenai Fjords National Park,** and the **Alaska Maritime National Wildlife Refuge.** The entire area is breathtaking, and you should not miss it in your haste to get to Anchorage (most cruise ships visiting Anchorage dock in Seward).

Seward is one of Alaska's oldest and most scenic communities, set between high mountain ranges on one side and Resurrection Bay on the other. The city was named for U.S. Secretary of State William H. Seward, who was instrumental in arranging the purchase of Alaska from Russia in 1867. Resurrection Bay was named in 1791 by Russian fur trader and explorer Alexander Baranof. The town was established in 1903 by railroad surveyors as an ocean terminal and supply center. The biggest event in Seward's history came after the 1964 Good Friday earthquake—the strongest ever recorded in North America. The tidal wave that followed the quake devastated the town; fortunately, most residents saw the harbor drain almost entirely, knew the wave would follow, and ran to high ground. Since then the town has relied heavily on commercial fishing, and its harbor is important for shipping coal to Asia.

For cruise-ship passengers, historic downtown Seward retains its small-town atmosphere; many of its buildings date from the early 1900s. Modern-day explorers can enjoy wildlife cruises, sportfishing, sailing, and kayaking in the bay, or investigate the intricacies of marine biology at the **Alaska SeaLife Center.**

If you're in Seward on the 4th of July, you'll have the chance to see—and perhaps join—the second-oldest footrace in North America. Each year, participants race straight up the 3,022-ft trail on Mt. Marathon from downtown. (*See* Hiking, *below.*)

Coming Ashore

Cruise ships dock within ½ mi (1 km) of downtown. The Seward Chamber of Commerce has a visitor information center at the cruise ship dock that is staffed when ships are in port. The Kenai Fjords National Park visitor center (tel. 907/224–3175) is within walking distance: turn left as you leave the pier, then left again onto 4th Avenue; the center is two blocks ahead. It's open daily 8 AM to 7 PM. Ask here about visiting scenic Exit Glacier, which is 13 mi (21 km) northwest of Seward. The Alaska National Historical Society operates a book and gift store in the Park Service center. The Chugach National Forest Ranger District office is at 334 4th Avenue.

The **Seward Trolley** (tel. 907/224–8051) stops at the cruise ship dock every half hour and heads to Seward's various points of interest. The cost is $1.50 one-way or $3 round-trip.

Exploring Seward

Seward's newest attraction is the **Alaska SeaLife Center,** right in town at the south end of 4th Avenue. Funded largely from the 1989 *Exxon Valdez* oil spill settlement, this facility covers a seven-acre site facing Resurrection Bay. Inside, you can watch scientists as they study everything from the genetics of herring to Steller sea lion telemetry. The emphasis is on wildlife research, rehabilitation, and education. No leaping killer whales here, but the centerpieces are the re-created sea and shore habitats—complete with underwater viewing windows—that are home to seals, sea lions, marine birds, salmon, and other animals. *Tel. 800/224–2525 or 907/ 224–6300. Admission: $12.50. Open daily in summer.*

Although most cruise-ship passengers head into Anchorage, there's a great deal to be seen in the Seward area. Don't miss the fjords in Resurrection Bay, with their bird rookeries and sea-lion haulouts. There are numerous tours to choose from—just check out the boardwalk area adjacent to the docks. **Kenai Fjords Tours** (tel. 907/224–8068 or 800/478–8068) has a very good half-day cruise of the bay with a stop for a salmon bake on Fox Island ($74 for a 5-hour lunch cruise). Other tour companies include **Mariah Charters** (tel. 907/224–8623 or 800/270–1238), **Kenai Coastal Tours** (tel. 907/224–8068 or 800/770–9119), **Alaska Renown Charters** (tel. 907/224–3806 or 800/655–3806),

Fresh Aire Charters (tel. 907/272–2755), and **Major Marine Tours** (tel. 907/224–8030 or 800/764–7300).

Thirteen miles (21 kilometers) northeast of Seward, **Exit Glacier** is the only road-accessible part of Kenai Fjords National Park. It's an easy ½ mi (1 km) hike to Exit Glacier from the parking lot; the first ¼ mi (½ km) is paved, which makes it accessible to those using wheelchairs.

If you're looking for history rather than scenery and wildlife, check out the **Seward Museum,** which has exhibits on the 1964 earthquake; the Iditarod Trail, the route of the 1925 diphtheria serum run from Seward to Nome (now commemorated by an annual 1,100 mi dogsled race); and Native history. *Corner of 3rd and Jefferson, tel. 907/224–3902. Admission: $2. Open daily 9–5.*

Across from the museum is the **1916 Rail Car Seward.** Once part of the Alaska's Railroad's rolling stock, it is now permanently parked here as an information center. Displays inside detail the 1964 Good Friday earthquake and how it devastated the town of Seward.

Shopping

Local gift and souvenir shops include the **Alaska Shop** (210 4th Ave., tel. 907/224–5420), **Bardarson Studio** (Small Boat Harbor, tel. 907/224–5448), and **Brown & Hawkins** (209 4th Ave., tel. 907/224–3011), Seward's oldest store. One of the best shopping options is **Resurrect Art Coffeehouse Gallery** (320 3rd Ave., tel. 907/224–7161; *see* Dining, *below*), where you'll find jewelry, pottery, books, prints, and paintings by local artisans.

Ranting Raven Bakery (228 4th Ave., tel. 907/224–2228) has a gift shop stocked with Russian and Ukrainian imports. Don't neglect to try the home-baked breads, pastries, and cakes.

Sports

FISHING

Every August the **Seward Silver Salmon Derby** attracts hundreds of folks who compete for the $10,000 top prize. For fishing, sightseeing, and drop-off/pickup tours, contact the **Fish House** (tel. 907/224–3674 or 800/257–7760), Seward's oldest operator.

HIKING

The strenuous **Mt. Marathon** trail starts at the west end of Lowell Canyon Road and runs practically straight uphill. An easier and more convenient hike for cruise passengers is the **Two Lakes Trail,** a loop of footpaths and bridges on the edge of town. A map is available from the Seward Chamber of Commerce (3rd Ave. and Jeffereson St., tel. 907/224–8051).

Dining

$$ **Ray's Waterfront.** When it comes to seafood, Ray's is the place. The walls are lined with trophy fish, and the windows front the busy harbor. It's a favorite place to grab a bite to eat while waiting for your tour boat or to relax with a cocktail as the sun goes down. The menu includes delicious mesquite-grilled salmon, plus clam chowder, crab, and other fresh-from-the-sea specialties. *On the Small Boat Harbor, tel. 907/224–5606. AE, D, DC, MC, V.*

$–$$ **Harbor Dinner Club & Lounge.** Stop at this spot in Seward's historic downtown district for solid lunch fare including burgers, sandwiches, and clam chowder. The outside deck is a good place to dine on a sunny summer afternoon. *220 5th Ave., tel. 907/224–3012. AE, D, DC, MC, V.*

$ **Resurrect Art Coffeehouse Gallery.** Built in 1916-17, it served for many years as a Lutheran church. Today, locals and tourists come to worship the espresso coffee and pastries on rainy days or the live music and poetry on summer evenings. *320 3rd Ave., tel. 907/224–7161. No credit cards.*

Sitka

Sitka was home to Tlingit people for centuries prior to the 18th-century arrival of the Russians. But Sitka's protected harbor, mild climate, and economic potential caught the attention of outsiders. Russian territorial governor Alexander Baranof saw in the island's massive timbered forests raw materials for shipbuilding, and its location suited trading routes to California, Hawaii, and the Orient. In 1799 Baranof established an outpost that he called Redoubt St. Michael, 6 mi (10 km) north of the present town, and moved a large number of his Russian and Aleut fur hunters there from Kodiak Island.

The Tlingits attacked Baranof's people and burned his buildings in 1802, but Baranof returned in 1804 with formidable strength, including shipboard cannons. He attacked the Tlingits at their fort near Indian River (site of the present-day, 105-acre Sitka National Historical Park) and drove them to the other side of the island. The Tlingits and Russians made peace in 1821, and, eventually the capital of Russian America was shifted from Kodiak to Sitka.

Today Sitka is known primarily for its onion-dome Russian Orthodox church, one of Southeast Alaska's most famous landmarks, and the Alaska Raptor Rehabilitation Center, a hospital for injured bald eagles and other birds of prey. Don't miss the 15 totem poles scattered around the grounds of the national historical park.

Coming Ashore

Only the smallest excursion vessels can dock at Sitka. Ocean liners must drop anchor in the harbor and tender passengers ashore near Centennial Hall, with its big Tlingit war canoe out front. Inside are an interesting local museum and the **Sitka Visitors Bureau** information desk (tel. 907/747–5940), which provides maps and brochures.

Sitka is hilly, but the waterfront attractions are an easy walk from the tender landing. You may, however, want to consider a taxi if you're heading all the way to the raptor center.

Exploring Sitka

Numbers in the margin correspond to points of interest on the Sitka map.

For one of the best views in town, turn left on Harbor Drive
❶ and head for **Castle Hill,** where Alaska was handed over to the United States on October 18, 1867, and where the first 49-star U.S. flag was flown on January 3, 1959, signifying the spirit of Alaska's statehood. Take the first right off Harbor Drive, then look for the entrance to Baranof Castle Hill State Historic Site. Make a left on the wheelchair-accessible path that takes you to the top of the hill overlooking Crescent Harbor.

❷ The **Sitka State Pioneers' Home,** which is hard to miss with its yellow paint and red roof, was built in 1934 as the

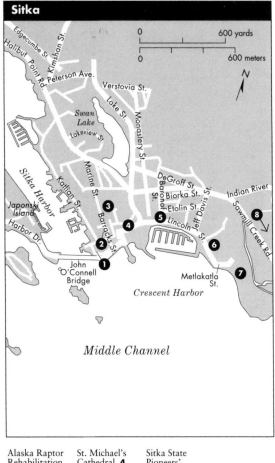

Sitka

0 — 600 yards
0 — 600 meters

N

Alaska Raptor Rehabilitation Center, **8**

Castle Hill, **1**

Russian Bishop's House, **5**

Russian and Lutheran Cemetery, **3**

St. Michael's Cathedral, **4**

Sheldon Jackson Museum, **6**

Sitka National Historical Park Visitor Center, **7**

Sitka State Pioneers' Home, **2**

first of several state-run retirement homes and medical-care facilities. The statue, symbolizing the state's Sourdoughs (as old-timers are nicknamed), was modeled after an authentic pioneer, William "Skagway Bill" Fonda. It portrays a determined prospector with pack, pick, rifle, and supplies, headed for gold country. *Corner of Katlian and Lincoln Sts.*

Three old anchors, believed to be from 19th-century British ships, mark **Totem Square**, across the street from the Pioneers' Home. Notice the double-headed eagle of czarist Russia on the park's totem pole. Just up the street from the Pioneers' Home is the **Sheet'ka Kwaan Naa Kahidi Community House** (456 Katlian St., tel. 907/747–7290), which schedules demonstrations and performances by members of the Sitka tribe. A small museum here houses historic prints and displays on edible plants.

❸ The most distinctive grave in the **Russian and Lutheran cemetery** marks the final resting place of Princess Maksoutoff, one of the most well-known members of the Russian royal family buried on Alaskan soil.

❹ Sitka's most photographed sight, **St. Michael's Cathedral,** had its origins in a frame-covered log structure built in the 1840s. In 1966 the church burned in a fire that swept through the business district. Using original blueprints, an almost exact replica of St. Michael's was built and dedicated in 1976. *Lincoln St., tel. 907/747–8120. Admission: $1 donation requested. Open daily 7:30–5:30 and when cruise ships are in port.*

❺ Several blocks past St. Michael's Cathedral on Lincoln Street and facing the harbor is the **Russian Bishop's House.** Constructed in 1842, this is one of the few remaining Russian log structures in Alaska. The Park Service has carefully restored the building, using original Russian furnishings and artifacts. In one room a portion of the house's interior has been peeled away to expose 19th-century construction techniques. *Lincoln St., tel. 907/747– 6281. Admission: $3. Open daily 9–1 and 2–5.*

❻ The octagonal **Sheldon Jackson Museum,** built in 1895, contains priceless Native American items collected by Dr. Sheldon Jackson from the remote regions of Alaska. Carved masks, Chilkat blankets, dogsleds, kayaks—even the helmet worn by Chief Katlean during the 1804 battle between the Sitka Tlingits and the Russians—are displayed here. *Lincoln St., tel. 907/747–8981. Admission: $3. Open daily 8–5.*

❼ The **Sitka National Historical Park Visitor Center** is at the far end of Lincoln Street. Audiovisual programs and exhibits, including Native and Russian artifacts, give an overview of Southeast Alaskan cultures, both old and new. Native artists and craftspeople are on hand to demonstrate and interpret traditional crafts of the Tlingit people, such as silversmithing, weaving, and basketry. A self-guided trail (maps available at the visitor center) to the site of the Tlingit Fort passes by some of the most skillfully carved totem poles in the state; several of these 15 poles date back almost a century. *Tel. 907/747–6281. Admission free. Open daily 8–5.*

❽ One of Sitka's most interesting attractions is the **Alaska Raptor Rehabilitation Center,** where injured birds of prey are nursed back to health. A visit to this unusual nature center rarely disappoints. *1101 Sawmill Creek Rd., tel. 907/ 747–8662. Admission and detailed tour $10. Open daily 8–5, and when cruise ships are in port.*

Shopping

Impressions (239 Lincoln St., tel. 907/747–5502 or 888/ 747– 5502) is a fine downtown gallery with art prints and limited editions from Southeast Alaskan artists. A few doors away, **Fairweather Prints** (209 Lincoln St., tel. 907/ 747–8677) sells beautifully printed "wearable art" with Alaskan designs. Native jewelry and other handicrafts are available from the **Sitka National Historical Park Visitor Center** (*see* Exploring Sitka, *above*).

A few stores, such as the **Russian-American Company** (407 Lincoln St., tel. 907/747–6228) and the **New Archangel Trading Co.** (335 Harbor Dr., across from Centennial Hall, tel. 907/747–8181), sell imported Russian items, including the popular *matruchka* nesting dolls.

For books on Alaska, stop by **Old Harbor Books** (201 Lincoln St., tel. 907/747–8808).

Sports

FISHING

Fishing is excellent here; see the information desk in Centennial Hall (*see* Coming ashore, *above*) for a list of local charter operators.

HIKING

Sitka's easiest hiking can be done along the 2 mi (3 km) of trails in **Sitka National Historical Park.** Here you can find some of the most dramatically situated totem poles in Alaska, relax at the picnic areas, and watch spawning salmon during the seasonal runs on the Indian River.

SEA KAYAKING

Several local companies offer guided sea-kayak trips, but you won't go wrong with **Baidarka Boats** (above Old Harbor Books at 201 Lincoln St., tel. 907/747–8996). Half-day trips are $50 per person. Be sure to make arrangements in advance so that your guide and/or kayak is waiting for you at the harbor.

Dining

$ Backdoor Cafe. For a dose of Sitka's caffeine-fueled hip side, scoot on through Old Harbor Books to this cozy latte joint with good pastries and bagels. *201 Lincoln St., tel. 907/ 747–8856. No credit cards.*

$ Bay View Restaurant. The Bay View, which is conveniently located for passengers touring the historic waterfront, has Russian specialties that reflect Sitka's colonial heritage. Gourmet burgers (including one with caviar) and deli sandwiches are also available, as are beer and wine. *407 Lincoln St., tel. 907/747– 5440. AE, MC, V.*

Saloons

Pioneer Bar (212 Katlean St., tel. 907/747–3456), across from the harbor, is a hangout for local fisherfolk. Tourists get a kick out of its authentic Alaskan ambience; the walls are lined with pictures of local fishing boats.

Skagway

The early Gold Rush days of Alaska, when dreamers and hooligans descended on the Yukon via the murderous White Pass, are preserved in Skagway. Now a part of the Klondike

Gold Rush National Historical Park, downtown Skagway was once the picturesque but sometimes lawless gateway for the frenzied stampede to the interior goldfields.

Local park rangers and residents now interpret and re-create that remarkable era for visitors. Old false-front stores, saloons, brothels, and wood sidewalks have been completely restored. You'll be regaled with tall tales of con artists, golden-hearted "ladies," stampeders, and newsmen. Such colorful characters as outlaw Jefferson "Soapy" Smith and his gang earned the town a reputation so bad that, by the spring of 1898, the superintendent of the Northwest Royal Mounted Police had labeled Skagway "little better than a hell on earth." But Soapy was killed in a duel with surveyor Frank Reid, and soon a civilizing influence, in the form of churches and family life, prevailed. When the gold played out just a few years later, the town of 20,000 dwindled to its current population of just over 700 (twice that in the summer months).

Coming Ashore

Cruise ships dock just a short stroll from downtown Skagway. From the pier you can see the large yellow-and-red White Pass & Yukon Railroad Depot, now the National Park Service Visitor Center. Step inside to view the historical photographs and a fine documentary video. Rangers lead frequent historical walks, and can provide details on nearby hiking trails and the Gold Rush cemetery. Information on other local attractions is available from the **Skagway Visitor Information Center** (333 5th Ave., ½ block off Broadway, tel. 907/983–2855 or 888/762–1898).

Virtually all the shops and Gold Rush sights are along Broadway, the main strip that leads from the visitor center through the middle of town, so you really don't need a taxi. Horse-drawn surreys, antique limousines, and modern vans pick up passengers at the pier and along Broadway for tours. The tracks of the White Pass and Yukon Railway run right along the pier; train departures are coordinated with cruise ship arrivals.

Exploring Skagway

Numbers in the margin correspond to points of interest on the Skagway map.

Skagway is perhaps the easiest port in Alaska to explore on foot. Just walk up and down Broadway, detouring here and there into the side streets. Keep an eye out for the humorous architectural details and advertising irreverence that mark the Skagway spirit.

❶ From the cruise ship dock, follow the road into town to the **Red Onion Saloon,** where a lady-of-the-evening mannequin peers down from the former second-floor brothel, and drinks are still served on the original mahogany bar. *Broadway and 2nd Ave., tel. 907/983–2222.*

❷ You can't help but notice the **Arctic Brotherhood Hall/Trail of '98 Museum,** with its curious driftwood-mosaic facade. On display in the museum are documents relating to Soapy Smith and Frank Reid, gambling paraphernalia from the old Board of Trade Saloon, Native artifacts, and more. *Broadway between 2nd Ave. and 3rd Ave., tel. 907/983–2420. Open when cruise ships are in port.*

❸ A small, almost inconsequential shack on 2nd Avenue was **Soapy's Parlor**—named after the notorious Gold Rush con man—but it's not open to tourists. *Off Broadway.*

❹ You'll find down-home sourdough cooking at the **Golden North Hotel.** Alaska's oldest hotel was built in 1898 and retains its Gold Rush–era appearance. Take a stroll through the lobby even if you don't plan to eat here. *Broadway and 3rd Ave., tel. 907/983–2451.*

❺ A rip-roaring revue, "Skagway in the Days of '98," is staged at the **Eagles Hall.** *Broadway and 6th Ave., tel. 907/ 983–2545. Admission: $14. Performances scheduled when cruise ships are in port.*

Shopping

Broadway is filled with numerous curio shops selling unusual merchandise. Although prices tend to be high as a general rule, good deals can be found, so shop around and don't buy the first thing you see.

Dedman's Photo Shop (Broadway between 3rd and 4th Aves., tel. 907/983–2353) has been a Skagway institution since the early days; here you'll find unusual historical photos, guidebooks, and old-fashioned newspapers.

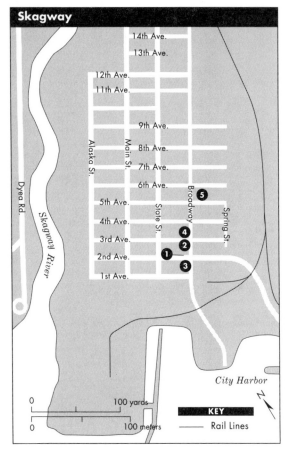

Skagway

14th Ave.
13th Ave.
12th Ave.
11th Ave.
9th Ave.
8th Ave.
7th Ave.
6th Ave.
5th Ave.
4th Ave.
3rd Ave.
2nd Ave.
1st Ave.

Dyea Rd.

Skagway River

Alaska St.

Main St.

State St.

Broadway

Spring St.

City Harbor

0   100 yards
0   100 meters

KEY
— Rail Lines

Arctic Brotherhood Hall/Trail of '98 Museum, **2**
Eagles Hall, **5**
Golden North Hotel, **4**
Red Onion Saloon, **1**
Soapy's Parlor, **3**

Sports

HIKING

Real wilderness is within a stone's throw of the docks, which makes this an excellent hiking port. Try the short jaunt to beautiful **Lower Dewey Lake.** Start at the corner of 4th Avenue and Spring Street, go toward the mountain, cross the footbridge over Pullen Creek, and follow the trail uphill. It's a 20-minute climb to the lake.

A less strenuous hike is the trip through **Gold Rush Cemetery,** where the epitaphs offer strange but lively bits of social commentary. Infamous villain Soapy Smith has a simple marker; hero Frank Reid has a much larger monument. To get to the cemetery, keep walking up Broadway, turn left onto 8th Avenue, then right onto State Street. Go through the railroad yards and follow the signs to the cemetery, which is 1½ mi (3 km), or a 30- to 45-minute walk, from town. To reach 300-ft-high **Reid Falls,** continue through the cemetery for ¼ mi (½ km). The National Park Service Visitor Center offers trail maps, advice, and the helpful brochure, *Skagway Gold Rush Cemetery Guide.* Trail maps are also available at the Skagway Visitor Center (*see* Coming Ashore, *above*).

Dining

$$–$$$ **Olivia's at the Skagway Inn.** Centrally located in the historic district, this is Skagway's upmarket restaurant, with a menu that specializes in freshly caught seafood. For lunch, they also serve up a delicious homemade potpie filled with seafood, chicken, or beef. Olivia's has a great wine and dessert selection. *7th Ave. and Broadway, tel. 907/983–3287 or 800/752–4929. MC, V.*

$–$$ **Golden North Restaurant.** To eat in the Golden North Hotel's dining room is to return to the days of Gold Rush con man Soapy Smith, heroic Frank Reid, and scores of pioneers, stampeders, and dance-hall girls. The decor is authentic and has been tastefully restored. The restaurant specializes in steaks and seafood, including fresh king crab from local waters. Also inside is a microbrewery that uses century-old beer recipes from the original Skagway Brewing Company. *3rd Ave. and Broadway, tel. 907/983– 2294. AE, DC, MC, V.*

Saloons

Moe's Frontier Bar (Broadway between 4th and 5th streets, tel. 907/983–2238), a longtime fixture on the Skagway scene, is a bar much frequented by the local folk.

At the **Red Onion** (Broadway at 2nd St., tel. 907/983–2222) you'll meet as many locals as you will visitors. There's live music on Thursday nights, ranging from rock and jazz to folk and acoustic. The upstairs was a gold-rush brothel.

Tracy Arm

Like Misty Fjords (*see above*), Tracy Arm and its sister fjord, Endicott Arm, have become staples on many Inside Passage cruises. Ships sail into the arm just before or after a visit to Juneau, the state capital, 50 mi (80 km) to the north. A day of scenic cruising in Tracy Arm is a lesson in geology and the forces that shaped Alaska. The fjord was carved by a glacier eons ago, leaving behind sheer granite cliffs. Waterfalls continue the process of erosion that the glaciers began. Very small ships may nudge their bows under the waterfalls, so crew members can fill pitchers full of glacial runoff. It's a uniquely Alaskan refreshment. Tracy Arm's glaciers haven't disappeared, though, they've just receded, and at the very end of Tracy Arm you'll come to two of them, known collectively as the twin Sawyer Glaciers.

Valdez

Valdez, with its year-round ice-free port, was an entry point for people and goods going to the interior during the Gold Rush. Today that flow has been reversed, and Valdez Harbor is the southern terminus of the Trans-Alaska pipeline, which carries crude oil from Prudhoe Bay and surrounding oil fields nearly 800 mi (1,290 km) to the north.

Much of Valdez looks new because the business area was relocated and rebuilt after being destroyed by the devastating Good Friday earthquake in 1964. A few of the old buildings were moved to the new town site.

Many Alaskan communities have summer fishing derbies, but Valdez may hold the record for the number of such contests, stretching from late May into September for halibut and various runs of salmon. The Valdez Silver Salmon Derby begins in late July and runs the entire month of August. Fishing charters abound in this area of Prince William Sound, and for a good reason, too: these fertile waters provide some of the best saltwater sportfishing in all of Alaska.

Coming Ashore

Ships tie up at the world's largest floating container dock. About 3 mi (5 km) from the heart of town, the dock is used not only for cruise ships, but also for loading cargo ships with timber and other products bound for markets "outside" (that's what Alaskans call the rest of the world).

Ship-organized motor coaches meet passengers on the pier and provide transportation into town. Cabs and car-rental services will also provide transportation from the pier. Several local ground and adventure-tour operators meet passengers as well.

Once in town, you'll find that Valdez is a very compact community. Almost everything is within easy walking distance of the Valdez Convention and Visitors Bureau in the heart of town. Motor coaches drop passengers at the Visitor Information Center.Taxi service is available and individualized tours of the area can be arranged with the cab dispatcher.

Exploring Valdez

Other than visiting the oil-pipeline terminal, which must be done on a tour, sightseeing in Valdez is mostly limited to gazing at the 5,000-ft mountain peaks surrounding the town or visiting the **Valdez Museum.** It depicts the lives, livelihoods, and events significant to Valdez and surrounding regions. Exhibits include a 1907 steam fire engine, a 19th-century saloon, and a model of the pipeline terminus. *217 Egan Ave., tel. 907/835–2764. Admission: $3. Open daily 9–6.*

Dining

$–$$ **Mike's Palace.** This busy restaurant with typical Italian-diner decor serves great pizzas, lasagna, beer-batter halibut, and Greek specialties, including gyros. *On the harbor, 201 N. Harbor Dr., tel. 907/835–2365. MC, V.*

Vancouver, British Columbia

Cosmopolitan Vancouver, Canada's answer to San Francisco, enjoys a spectacular setting. Tall fir trees stand practically downtown, rock spires tower close by, the ocean laps at your doorstep, and people from every corner of the earth create a youthful and vibrant atmosphere.

Vancouver is a young city, even by North American standards. It was not yet a town in 1871, when British Columbia became part of the Canadian confederation. The city's history, such as it is, remains visible to the naked eye: eras are stacked east to west along the waterfront like some century-old archaeological dig—from cobblestoned, late-Victorian Gastown to shiny postmodern glass cathedrals of commerce grazing the sunset.

Note that Vancouver is usually the first or last stop on a cruise, unless you're sailing on a longer cruise that begins in Los Angeles or San Francisco.

Coming Ashore

Most ships dock downtown at the Canada Place cruise-ship terminal—instantly recognizable by its rooftop of dramatic white sails and a few minutes walk from the city center. A few vessels tie up at the Ballantyne cruise terminal, a 10- to 15-minute, $12 cab ride from the downtown core. A third pier under construction to the east of Canada Place will be ready by 2003. Stop off at the Tourism Vancouver Infocentre (tel. 604/683–2000) next door to the Waterfront Centre Hotel and across the street from Canada Place to pick up brochures on Vancouver attractions and events before leaving the pier area.

Many sights of interest are concentrated in the hemmed-in peninsula of Downtown Vancouver. The heart of Vancouver—which includes the downtown area, Stanley Park, and the West End high-rise residential neighborhood—sits on this peninsula bordered by English Bay and the Pacific Ocean to the west; by False Creek, the inlet home to Granville Island, to the south; and by Burrard Inlet, the working port of the city, to the north, past which loom the North Shore mountains. The oldest part of the city—Gastown and Chinatown—lies at the edge of Burrard Inlet.

It is difficult to hail a cab in Vancouver; unless you're near a hotel, you'd have better luck calling a taxi service. Try **Yellow** (tel. 604/681–3311) or **Black Top** (tel. 604/681–2181).

Exploring Vancouver

Numbers in the margin correspond to points of interest on the Downtown Vancouver map. Prices are given in Canadian dollars.

① At **Canada Place,** walk along the promenade around the pier for fine views of the Burrard Inlet harbor and Stanley Park.

② The **Canadian Craft Museum,** which opened in 1992, is one of the first national cultural facilities dedicated to crafts—historical and contemporary, functional and decorative. Examples here range from elegantly carved utensils with decorative handles to colorful hand-spun and handwoven garments. *639 Hornby St., tel. 604/687–8266. Admission: $5. Open Mon.–Wed. and Fri.–Sat. 10–5, Thurs. 10–9, Sun. noon–5. Closed Tues. Sept.–Apr.*

③ **Gastown** is where Vancouver originated after "Gassy" Jack Deighton arrived at Burrard Inlet in 1867 with his Native American wife, a barrel of whiskey, and few amenities and set up a saloon to entertain the scattered loggers and trappers living in the area. When the transcontinental train arrived in 1887, Gastown became the transfer point for trade with the Orient and was soon crowded with hotels and warehouses. The Klondike Gold Rush encouraged further development until 1912, when the "Golden Years" ended. From the 1930s to the 1950s hotels were converted into rooming houses, and the warehouse district shifted elsewhere. The neglected area gradually became run-down. However, both Gastown and Chinatown were declared historic districts in the late 1970s and have been revitalized. Gastown is now chockablock with boutiques, cafés, and souvenir shops.

④ The Chinese were among the first inhabitants of Vancouver, and some of the oldest buildings in the city are in **Chinatown.** There was already a sizable Chinese community in British Columbia because of the 1858 Cariboo Gold Rush in central British Columbia, but the greatest influx from China came in the 1880s, during construction of the Canadian Pacific Railway, when 15,000 laborers arrived.

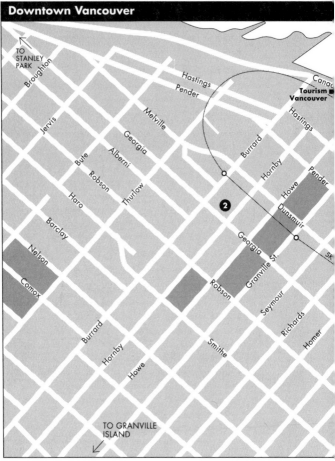

Downtown Vancouver

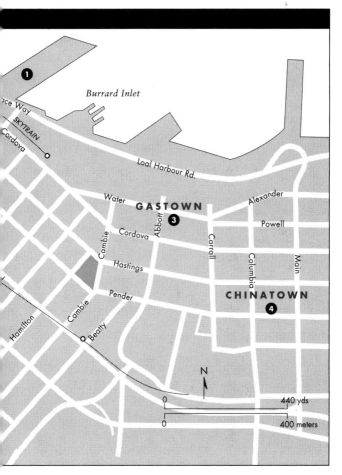

Highlights of a visit to Chinatown include the **Dr. Sun Yat-Sen Classical Chinese Garden** (578 Carrall St., tel. 604/689–7133), the first authentic Ming Dynasty–style garden built outside of China, and the **Chinese Cultural Centre Museum and Archives** (555 Columbia St., tel. 604/687–0282), an art gallery and museum dedicated to Chinese-Canadian culture.

The fastest route from Gastown to Chinatown passes through a rough part of town, so it's better to take a taxi between the two areas or, if you prefer to walk, take the long way around, south on Cambie and east on Pender.

Stanley Park is a 1,000-acre wilderness park just blocks from the downtown section of the city. An afternoon in Stanley Park gives you a capsule tour of Vancouver that includes beaches, the ocean, the harbor, Douglas fir and cedar forests, and a good look at the North Shore mountains. The park sits on a peninsula, and along the shore is a pathway 9 km (6 mi) long, called the seawall. You can drive or bicycle all the way around. Bicycles are for rent at Georgia and Denman streets near the park entrance. Cyclists must wear helmets, ride in a counterclockwise direction, and stay on their side of the path. Between mid-May and mid-September, a shuttle bus (tel. 604/257–8400) provides regular service around the park.

Inside the park are several restaurants, a children's miniature railway, two sandy beaches, and a network of trails through old-growth forest. At the **Vancouver Aquarium** (tel. 604/659–3474), within the park grounds, you can see whale shows and sealife from around the world.

Taxis to Stanley Park cost about $8 one way from Gastown or Chinatown (*see* Coming Ashore, *above*, for taxi companies). You can also catch a westbound bus on Hastings Street (make sure you are west of the cross street Cambie). The bus is marked STANLEY PARK, and the fare is C$1.50 each way. For information, call 604/521–0400.

Granville Island A 15-minute cab ride or a short hop on a foot-passenger ferry (tel. 604/689–5858 or 604/684–7781) will take you to this island in False Creek south of downtown. A former industrial area refurbished in the 1970s as an urban park, it's now one of Vancouver's liveliest spots, with a huge public market, art galleries and craft shops, and

In case you want to see the world.

At American Express, we're here to make your journey a smooth one. So we have over 1,700 travel service locations in over 130 countries ready to help. What else would you expect from the world's largest travel agency?

do more **AMERICAN EXPRESS**

Travel

In case you want to be welcomed there.

We're here to see that you're always welcomed at establishments everywhere. That's why millions of people carry the American Express® Card – for peace of mind, confidence, and security, around the world or just around the corner.

do more

Cards

To apply, call 1 800 THE-CARD
or visit www.americanexpress.com

In case you're running low.

We're here to help with more than 190,000 Express Cash locations around the world. In order to enroll, just call American Express at 1 800 CASH-NOW before you start your vacation.

do more

Express Cash

And in case you'd rather be safe than sorry.

We're here with American Express® Travelers Cheques. They're the safe way to carry money on your vacation, because if they're ever lost or stolen you can get a refund, practically anywhere or anytime. To find the nearest place to buy Travelers Cheques, call 1 800 495-1153. Another way we help you do more.

do more

Travelers Cheques

several museums and theaters. Call the Granville Island Information Centre (604/666–5784) for information.

Shopping

Unlike many cities where suburban malls have taken over, Vancouver has a downtown that is still lined with individual boutiques and specialty shops. Stores are usually open daily and on Thursday and Friday nights, and Sunday noon to 5.

Save your receipts to receive a 7% GST tax refund from the Canadian government when you leave Canada. Ask for a form at customs; many Vancouver shops also have GST refund forms.

Robson Street, stretching from Burrard to Bute streets, is full of small boutiques and cafés. Vancouver's liveliest street is not only for the fashion-conscious; it also provides many excellent corners for people-watching and attracts an array of street performers.

Fashion shops can be found in and around **Sinclair Centre** (757 West Hastings at Granville), just a block south of the Canada Place cruise-ship terminal. Here you'll find top-of-the-line European designs at **Leone** (tel. 604/ 683–1133) and unique fashions inspired by Northwest Coast Native art at **Dorothy Grant** (tel. 604/681–0201).

Chinatown (*see* Exploring Vancouver, *above*)—centered on Pender and Main streets—is an exciting and animated area with restaurants, exotic foods, distinctive architecture, and import shops. **Ten Ren Tea and Ginseng Company** (550 Main St., tel. 604/684–1566) and **Ten Lee Hong Tea and Ginseng** (500 Main St., tel. 604/689–7598) carry every kind of tea imaginable. For art, ceramics, and rosewood furniture, take a look at **Yeu Hua Handicraft Ltd.** (173 E. Pender, tel. 604/662–3832). If you are staying overnight on a weekend, check out the **Chinatown Night Market**—a street market running from 6:30 to 11 PM Friday, Saturday, and Sunday evenings from May to September—along the 200 blocks of Keefer and Pender streets.

For books, **Chapters** (788 Robson St., tel. 604/682–4066) and **Duthie's** (710 Granville St., tel. 604/689–1802) have excellent selections of books and magazines. In both stores you can buy Canadian and British editions of books that may be hard to find in the States.

Some of the best places in Vancouver for good-quality souvenirs (West Coast Native art, books, music, jewelry, and so on) are the **Gallery Shop** (in the Vancouver Art Gallery, 750 Hornby St., tel. 604/662–4706), the **Canadian Craft Museum gift shop** (639 Hornby St., tel. 604/687–8266), and the **Clamshell Gift Shop** at the aquarium in Stanley Park (tel. 604/659–3413). In Gastown, Northwest Coast Native art is available at **Images for a Canadian Heritage** (164 Water St., tel. 604/685–7046) and **Hill's Indian Crafts** (165 Water St., tel. 604/685–4249).

Sports

BIKING

Vancouver's 10-mile Seawall bicycle path starts at Canada Place and continues, with a few detours, around Stanley Park and False Creek to the south shore of English Bay. **Stanley Park** (*see* Exploring, *above*) is the most popular spot for family cycling. Rentals are available near the park entrance from Bayshore Bicycles (745 Denman St., tel. 604/688–2453) or Spokes Bicycle Rentals (1798 W. Georgia, tel. 604/688–5141).

GOLF

For a spur-of-the-moment game, call **Last Minute Golf** (tel. 604/878–1833). The company matches golfers and courses at substantial greens fees discounts. The half-day packages offered by **West Coast Golf Shuttle** (tel. 604/878–6800) include the greens fee, a power cart, and hotel pick-up. Two of the more exciting local courses are the **Furry Creek Golf and Country Club** (Hwy. 99, Furry Creek, tel. 604/922–9576), a mountain- and ocean-view course about 45 minutes north of Vancouver, and the **Westwood Plateau Golf and Country Club** (3251 Plateau Blvd., Coquitlam, tel. 604/552–0777), a mountainside course about 45 minutes east of town.

Dining

Most of these restaurants are popular, and reservations are recommended. Diners without reservations won't be turned away, but may have to wait in line. Pubs listed below usually serve snacks.

$$ Aqua Riva. This lofty, lively modern Art Deco room just yards from the Canada Place cruise-ship terminal affords striking views over the harbor and the North Shore mountains. Food from the wood-fired oven, rotisserie, and grill includes thin-crust pizzas with innovative toppings, grilled salmon, spit-roasted chicken, and a good selection of pastas, salads, and sandwiches. There's a long microbrew and martini list, too. *200 Granville St., tel. 604/683–5599. AE, D, DC, MC, V.*

$$ Imperial Chinese Seafood. This elegant Cantonese restaurant in the Art Deco Marine Building offers stupendous views through two-story floor-to-ceiling windows of Stanley Park and the North Shore mountains across Coal Harbour. Any dish featuring lobster, crab, or shrimp from the live tanks is recommended, as is the dim sum served every day from 11 to 2:30. *355 Burrard St., tel. 604/688–8191. AE, MC, V.*

$$ Raintree at the Landing. Set in a beautifully renovated heritage building in Gastown, Vancouver's first Pacific Northwest restaurant has waterfront views, fireplaces, and cuisine based on fresh, often organic, regional ingredients. The seasonal menus and specials incorporate innovative treatments of such local bounty as Salt Spring Island lamb and Fraser Valley rabbit, as well as luxurious soups, home-baked breads, a Pacific Northwest wine list, and a good selection of vegetarian entrées. *375 Water St., tel. 604/ 688–5570. AE, DC, MC, V.*

$ Hon's Wun-Tun House. Mr. Hon has been keeping Vancouverites in Chinese comfort food since the 1970s. The best bets on the 300-item menu (where nothing is over $10) are the potstickers (Chinese dumplings that come fried, steamed, or in soup), the won ton and noodle dishes, and anything with barbecued beef. The enormous Robson Street location has a separate kitchen for vegetarians and an army of servers to keep your tea topped up. The original Chinatown outlet is atmospherically steamy and crowded. *1339 Robson St., tel. 604/685–0871; 268 Keefer St. 604/ 688–0871. Reservations not accepted. MC, V.*

Bars and Lounges

The **Gerard Lounge** (845 Burrard St., tel. 604/682–5511) at the Sutton Place Hotel, with its Old World ambience, is probably the nicest in the city. The **900 West Wine Bar** (900 W. Georgia St., tel. 604/669–9378) in the Hotel Vancouver serves 55 wines by the glass. The **Bacchus Lounge** (845 Hornby St., tel. 604/-608–5319) in the Wedgewood Hotel is stylish and sophisticated. The **Garden Terrace** (791 W. Georgia St., tel. 604/689–9333) in the Four Seasons is bright and airy with greenery and a waterfall.

At **Steam Works** (375 Water St., tel. 604/689–2739), on the edge of bustling Gastown, they use an age-old steam brewing process and large copper kettles (visible through glass walls in the dining room downstairs) to whip up six to nine brews; the espresso ale is interesting. The **Yaletown Brewing Company** (1111 Mainland St., tel. 604/681–2739) is based in a huge renovated warehouse with a glassed-in brewery turning out eight tasty microbrews; it also has a darts and billiards pub and a restaurant with an open-grill kitchen.

Victoria, British Columbia

Though Victoria is not in Alaska, it is a port of call for many ships cruising the Inside Passage. Just like the communities of Southeast Alaska, Victoria had its own Gold Rush stampede in the 1800s, when 25,000 miners flocked to British Columbia's Cariboo country. Today the city is a mix of stately buildings and English traditions. Flower baskets hang from lampposts, shops sell Harris tweed and Irish linen, locals play cricket and croquet, and visitors sightsee aboard red double-decker buses or horse-drawn carriages. Afternoon tea is still served daily at the city's elegant Empress Hotel. No visit to Victoria is complete without a stroll through Butchart Gardens, a short drive outside the city.

Coming Ashore

Only the smallest excursion vessels can dock downtown in the Inner Harbour. Ocean liners must tie up at the Ogden Point Cruise Ship Terminal, a C$4–C$5 cab ride from downtown. Metered taxis meet the ship. The tourist visitor information center (812 Wharf St., tel. 250/953–2033) is in front of the Empress Hotel, midway along the Inner Harbour.

Most points of interest are within walking distance of the Empress Hotel. For those that aren't, public and private transportation is readily available from the Inner Harbour.

The public bus system is excellent as well. Pick up route maps and schedules at the tourist information office.

Taxi rates are C$2.15 for pickup, C$1.30 per km (½ mi). Contact **Bluebird** (tel. 250/382–2222) or **Victoria Taxi** (250/383–7111).

Exploring Victoria

Numbers in the margin correspond to points of interest on the Inner Harbour, Victoria, map. Prices are given in Canadian dollars.

❶ Victoria's heart is the **Inner Harbour,** always bustling with ferries, seaplanes, and yachts from all over the world.

❷ The ivy-covered 1908 **Empress Hotel** is the dowager of Victoria. High tea in this little patch of England is a local ritual. Scones and jam, pastries and tea are served in the elegant tea lobby every afternoon; reservations are required (call 250/389–2727) and a dress code calls for smart casual wear. *721 Government St., tel. 250/384–8111.*

❸ The **Crystal Garden** was built in 1925 under a glass roof as a public saltwater swimming pool. It has been renovated into a tropical conservatory and aviary, with flamingos, tortoises, macaws, and butterflies. *713 Douglas St., behind the Empress Hotel, tel. 250/381–1213. Admission: $7.50. Open July and Aug., daily 8:30–8; Nov.–mid-Apr., daily 10–4:30. Other months, daily 9–6.*

❹ **Thunderbird Park** displays a ceremonial longhouse (a communal dwelling) and a fine collection of totem poles. *Belleville St, beside the Royal British Columbia Museum.*

❺ Next to Thunderbird Park is the 1852 **Helmcken House,** the province's oldest residence, which has a display of antique medical instruments. *10 Elliot St., tel. 250/361–0021. Admission: $4. Open May–Sept., daily 10–5.*

❻ The superb **Royal British Columbia Museum** will take at least a couple of hours of your time: its exhibits encompass 12,000 years of natural and human history. *675 Belleville St., tel. 250/387–3014 or 800/661–5411. Admission: $7. Open daily 9–5.*

❼ The stately, neo-Gothic **British Columbia Parliament Buildings** were constructed of local stone and wood and opened

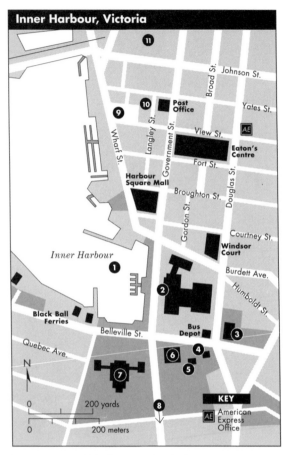

Inner Harbour, Victoria

Bastion Square, **9**

British Columbia Parliament Buildings, **7**

Crystal Garden, **3**

Emily Carr House, **8**

Empress Hotel, **2**

Helmcken House, **5**

Inner Harbour, **1**

Maritime Museum of British Columbia, **10**

Market Square, **11**

Royal British Columbia Museum, **6**

Thunderbird Park, **4**

in 1898. Atop the central dome is a gilded statue of Captain George Vancouver, for whom Vancouver Island was named. Free half-hour tours are offered several times a day in summer. *501 Belleville St., tel. 250/387–3046. Admission: free. Open June–Aug. daily 9–5; Sept.–May, weekdays 8:30–5.*

❽ The Victorian **Emily Carr House** was the childhood home of one of Canada's most famous and most beloved artists; the artist's autobiography was used to guide the restoration of the house. *207 Government St., tel. 250/383–5843. Admission: $5. Open mid-May–mid-Oct., daily 10–5.*

❾ Just a short walk from the Inner Harbour is **Bastion Square.** Follow Government Street to Humboldt Street. With the water to your left, bear left onto Wharf Street, and look for the square on your right. Laid out in 1843 as the original site of Ft. Victoria, the atmospheric square is now home to boutiques and restaurants.

On the north side of Bastion Square, the old courthouse is
❿ now the **Maritime Museum of British Columbia.** Completely renovated in 1998, it has three floors of nautical-theme exhibits, including a full-scale vice-admiralty courtroom and one of North America's oldest cage lifts. *28 Bastion Sq., tel. 250/385–4222. Admission: $5. Open daily 9:30–4:30.*

⓫ Two blocks north of Bastion Square is **Market Square,** a former staging post for prospectors on their way to the Klondike. It's now an atmospheric courtyard surrounded by two levels of boutiques and cafés. From Market Square, you can cut up Fan Tan Alley, Canada's narrowest street, to Victoria's historic Chinatown.

Take a taxi (or a shore excursion) to **Butchart Gardens.** In a city of gardens, these 50 acres rank among the most beautiful in the world. In July and August, a fireworks display is held every Saturday evening. *22 km (14 mi) north of Victoria on Hwy. 17, tel. 250/652–4422. Admission: $15.75. Open daily 9 AM–10:30 PM in summer.*

Shopping

Save your receipts to receive a 7% GST tax refund from the Canadian government when you leave Canada; ask for a form at customs. Victoria stores specializing in English imports are plentiful, though Canadian-made goods are usually a better buy.

Victoria's main shopping area is along Government Street north of the Empress Hotel. **Hill's Indian Crafts** (1008 Government St., tel. 250/385–3911) sells original West Coast Native artwork. For imported linens and lace, have a look at the **Irish Linen Stores** (1019 Government St., tel. 250/383–0321). **Munro's Books** (1108 Government St., tel. 250/382–2464), in a beautifully restored 1909 building, is one of Canada's prettiest bookstores. **The Cowichan Trading Co., Ltd.** (1328 Government St., tel. 250/383–0321) sells Northwest Coast Native jewelry, art, and hand-knit Cowichan sweaters.

From Government St. turn right onto Fort Street and walk four blocks to **Antique Row,** between Blanshard and Cook streets, where dozens of antiques shops sell books, jewelry, china, furniture, artwork, and collectibles.

Dining

$$ **Bengal Lounge.** Buffet lunches in the elegant Empress Hotel include curries with extensive condiment trays of coconut, nuts, cool *raita* (yogurt with mint or cucumber), and chutney. Lunch is served daily between 11:30 and 3. *721 Government St., tel. 250/384–8111. AE, D, DC, MC, V.*

$$ **Il Terrazzo.** The locals' choice for al fresco dining, Il Terrazzo has a charming redbrick terrace tucked away off Waddington Alley just north of the Inner Harbour. Grilled lamb chops on a bed of linguine and pizzas from the restaurant's wood-burning oven are among the hearty Italian dishes served. *555 Johnson St., off Waddington Alley (call for directions), tel. 250/361–0028. Reservations essential. AE, MC, V. No lunch Sun.*

Wrangell

Between Ketchikan and Petersburg lies Wrangell, on an island near the mouth of the mighty Stikine River. The town is off the typical cruise-ship track and is visited mostly by lines with an environmental or educational emphasis, such as Alaska Sightseeing or World Explorer Cruises. This small, unassuming timber and fishing community has lived under three flags since the arrival of the Russian traders.

Known as Redoubt St. Dionysius when it was part of Russian America, the town was renamed Fort Stikine after the British took it over. The name was changed to Wrangell when the Americans purchased it in 1867.

Coming Ashore

Cruise ships calling in Wrangell dock downtown, within walking distance of the museum and gift stores. Greeters welcome passengers and are available to answer questions. The chamber of commerce visitor center (tel. 907/874–3901 or 800/367–9745) is next to the dock inside the Stikine Inn.

Wrangell's few attractions—the most notable being totem-filled Chief Shakes Island—are within walking distance of the pier. To get to Petroglyph Beach, where you find rocks marked with mysterious prehistoric symbols, you'll need to take a shore excursion or hire a cab. Call **Porky's Cab Co.** (tel. 907/874– 3603) or **Star Cab** (tel. 907/874–3622).

Exploring Wrangell

Numbers in the margin correspond to points of interest on the Wrangell map.

❶ Walking up Front Street will bring you to **Kiksadi Totem Park,** a pocket park of Alaska greenery and impressive totem poles.

On your way to Wrangell's number-one attraction—Chief
❷ Shakes Island—stop at **Chief Shakes's grave site,** uphill from the Wrangell shipyard on Case Avenue. Buried here is Shakes VI, the last of a line of chiefs who bore that name. He led the local Tlingits during the first half of the 19th century. Two killer-whale totems mark the chief's burial place.

❸ On **Chief Shakes Island,** reached by a footbridge off the harbor dock, you can see some of the finest totem poles in Alaska, as well as a tribal house constructed in the 1930s as a replica of one that was home to many of the various Shakes and their peoples. You'll see six totems on the island, two of them more than 100 years old. The original corner posts of the tribal house are in the museum. The house is open for visitors when ships are in port. *Tel. 907/874– 3747. Admission: $1.50 donation requested.*

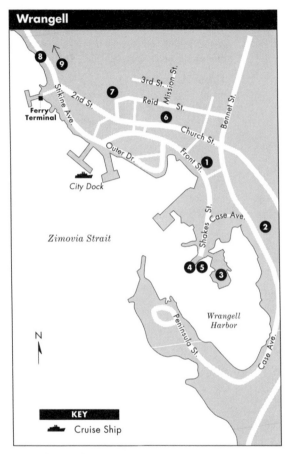

Wrangell

Ferry Terminal

City Dock

Zimovia Strait

Wrangell Harbor

N

KEY

Cruise Ship

Stikine Ave.
2nd St.
3rd St.
Mission St.
Reid St.
Bennet St.
Church St.
Front St.
Outer Dr.
Shakes St.
Case Ave.
Peninsula St.

After your visit to Chief Shakes Island, wander out to the end of the dock for the view and for picture taking at the

❹ ❺ **seaplane float** and **boat harbor.**

❻ The **Wrangell City Museum's** historical collection includes totem fragments, petroglyphs, and other Native artifacts; a bootlegger's still; a vintage 1800s Linotype and presses; and a cedar-bark basket collection. *318 Church St., tel. 907/ 874–3770. Admission: $2. Open summer weekdays 10– 5, Sat. 1–5, and when cruise ships are in port.*

❼ Outside the **public library** (124 2nd Ave., tel. 907/874– 3535) are a couple of ancient petroglyphs. They are worth seeing if you don't plan to make the trip to Petroglyph Beach (*see below*).

❽ To some, the artifacts that make up **"Our Collections,"** by owner Elva Bigelow, constitute less a museum than a garage sale waiting to happen. Still, large numbers of viewers seem quite taken by the literally thousands of unrelated collectibles (clocks, animal traps, waffle irons, tools, etc.) that the Bigelows have gathered in a half century of Alaska living. *Evergreen Ave., tel. 907/874–3646. Admission: Donations accepted. Call before setting out to visit.*

❾ **Petroglyph Beach** is undoubtedly one of the more curious sights in Southeast Alaska. Here, scattered among other rocks along the shore, are three dozen or more large stones bearing designs and pictures chiseled by unknown ancient artists. No one knows what they mean. Perhaps they were boundary markers or messages. Because the petroglyphs can be damaged by physical contact, the state discourages visitors from creating a "rubbing" off the rocks with rice paper and crayons. Instead, you can photograph the petroglyphs or purchase a rubber-stamp duplicate of selected petroglyphs from the city museum. Do not, of course, attempt to move any of the petroglyph stones.

Shopping

A unique souvenir from Wrangell is a natural garnet, gathered at Garnet Ledge, facing the Stikine River. The semiprecious gems are sold on the streets by the children of Wrangell for 50¢ to $50, depending on their size and quality.

Dining

$ Wrangell's dining options are limited, with no real stand-outs. Several local restaurants, including the **Stikine Inn** (107 Front St., tel. 907/874–3388) and **Diamond C Cafe** (214 Front St., tel. 907/874–3677), offer standard fill-you-up American fare. The best bet for visitors is probably **Waterfront Grill** (214 Front St., tel. 907/874–2353), serving homemade pizzas, salads, and burgers.

Ports of Embarkation and Disembarkation

San Francisco

The entire dock area of San Francisco is a tourist neighborhood of entertainment, shops, and restaurants called the Embarcadero. There's plenty to see and do within easy walking distance of the cruise-ship terminals. With your back to the cruise pier, turn right to get to Fisherman's Wharf, Ghirardelli Square, and the Maritime Museum. If you don't want to walk, Bus 32 travels along the Embarcadero. You can also pick up a ferry to Alcatraz at Pier 41.

LONG-TERM PARKING

A five-story public garage is one block from the cruise terminal at Pier 35. Parking is $8 per day.

FROM THE AIRPORT

San Francisco International Airport, one of the busiest in the country, is about 14 mi (22 km) from the cruise pier. A cab ride from the airport to the cruise pier costs a flat rate of $34 and takes 25–30 minutes, depending upon traffic. Less expensive ($12 per person) shuttle buses and shared stretch limousines can be picked up curbside at the airport, but they take longer. Make sure the shuttle or limousine will drop you off at the cruise pier.

Vancouver

Many travelers consider British Columbia's Vancouver one of the most beautiful cities in the world, so it is only appropriate that its cruise-ship terminal is also one of the most convenient and attractive. Right on the downtown waterfront, the Canada Place terminal is instantly recognizable by its rooftop of dramatic sails. Inside are shops and restaurants. Porters are courteous and taxis plentiful.

If you are early, consider visiting historic Gastown just a couple of blocks away (to the left if you have your back to the water).

Parking at **Citipark** (tel. 604/684–2251 for reservations) at Canada Place costs C$14 per day for cruise-ship passengers who pay in advance. Cheaper rates (less than C$10 a day) are available at certain hotels near the terminal, but you will need to take a cab between your car and the ship.

Vancouver International Airport is approximately 17½ km (11 mi) away from Canada Place, but the road weaves through residential neighborhoods instead of highways. A taxi from the airport costs about C$25 and takes about 25 minutes.

Cruise-line bus transfers from the Vancouver and Seattle airports are the most convenient, providing baggage handling and, for those with flights into Seattle, customs clearance. If for some reason you cannot connect with one of these buses, **Vancouver Airporter Service** (tel. 604/244–9888 or 800/668–3141) provides fast, frequent bus service between the Vancouver airport and the Pan Pacific Hotel at Canada Place for C$10 one-way, C$17 round-trip. From Seattle's SeaTac Airport, **Quick Shuttle** (tel. 604/244–3744 or 800/665–2122) makes the four- to five-hour bus trip for $35 one-way, $63 round-trip.

3 Shore Excursions

Shore excursions arranged by the cruise line are a very convenient way to see the sights, although you pay extra for this convenience. Before your cruise, you'll receive a booklet describing the shore excursions your cruise line offers. A few lines let you book excursions in advance; all sell them on board during the cruise. If you cancel your excursion, you may incur penalties, the amount varying with the number of days remaining until the tour. Because these trips are specialized, many have limited capacity and are sold on a first-come, first-served basis.

Among the many options available, there are some "musts." At least once during your cruise, try flightseeing—it's the only way you'll grasp the expansiveness and grandeur of the land. Go to an evening salmon feast, where you'll savor freshly caught fish cooked over an open fire in a natural setting. And experience an outdoor adventure—you don't have to be athletically inclined to raft down a river or paddle a sea-kayak along the coastline.

Because cruise-line shore-excursion booklets present such a great variety of options, we have compiled a selection below of the most worthwhile excursions to help you make your choices. Not all those listed below are offered by all cruise lines. Prices will vary. For more information on the cities and some of the attractions discussed, *see* Chapter 2.

You can also arrange many of these tours through the visitor-information counter in each port. These counters are usually close to the pier; for exact locations, *see* Coming Ashore *in each port of call section in* Chapter 2.

Haines

A small coastal community, Haines was originally settled by the Tlingit Indians. It is known for the work of its local artists, Native dancers, and, in the fall, lots of bald eagles.

Adventure

Glacier Flightseeing. If your cruise doesn't include a visit to Glacier Bay, here's a chance to see the glacial ice field from up high. The ice field is so thick in places it covers the surrounding mountains, whose peaks barely rise above the icy surface. *1¼ hrs. Cost: $125.*

Cultural

Chilkat Dancers. A drive through Ft. William Henry Seward includes a dance performance by the Chilkat Dancers, noted for their vivid tribal masks. Some lines combine this tour with a salmon bake. *3 hrs. Cost: $40–$60.*

Scenic

Chilkat River by Jet Boat. A cruise through the Chilkat Bald Eagle Preserve introduces you to some eagles and—if you're lucky—a moose or a bear. It is a smooth, rather scenic trip, but in summer, you'll see little wildlife. Come October, though, imagine the trees filled with up to 4,000 bald eagles. *3½ hrs. Cost: $70–$95.*

Tastes of Alaska

Haines Salmon Bake. Locally caught salmon is the main dish served "potlach-style" (a potlach is an elaborate feast) in a Native longhouse. *1 hr. Cost: $25.*

Juneau

This is Alaska's capital, where old and new mix in a frontier atmosphere. Juneau's historic center is easy to see on foot. Try to get to the Mendenhall Glacier, one of Alaska's "drive-up" glaciers, which is 13 mi outside town.

Adventure

Helicopter Glacier Trekking. This high-adventure excursion takes you deep into the ice field for glacier trekking with climbing boots, crampons, climbing harness, and ice-ax. *4–4½ hrs. Cost: $300– $350.*

Juneau Bike Tour. Glacial views and the sights and smells of the old-growth rain forest are among the highlights of this bicycle excursion, which usually covers about 10 mi. *3–4 hrs. Cost: $60.*

Mendenhall Glacier Helicopter Ride. One of the best helicopter glacier tours in Alaska includes a landing on an ice field for a walk on the glacier. Boots and rain gear are provided. *2½ hrs. Cost: $165.*

Mendenhall River Raft or Canoe Trip. This rafting trip goes down the Mendenhall River, with some stretches of gentle rapids. Professional rafters row, and rubber rain boots, protective clothing, and life jackets are provided. The minimum age is six years—and kids love this one. Another version of this excursion uses a Native-style canoe for a paddle across Mendenhall Lake in view of the glacier. *3½ hrs. Cost: $75–$100.*

Scenic
Gold Panning and Gold Mine Tour. You can pan for gold with a prospector guide and tour the entrance area of the Alaska-Juneau mine. This is great for kids. *1½ hrs. Cost: $40.*

Juneau Sights. If you don't opt for the helicopter tour, take this bus excursion to see the Mendenhall Glacier and spawning salmon at the local hatchery. *2½–3 hrs. Cost: $30–$40.*

Tastes of Alaska
Floatplane Ride and Taku Glacier Lodge Wilderness Salmon Bake. Fly over the Juneau Ice Field to Taku Glacier Lodge where you can dine on outstanding barbecued salmon. Afterward, explore the virgin rain forest or enjoy the rustic lodge. There's a large mosquito population here but repellent is available. The tour is expensive, but it consistently gets rave reviews. *3 hrs. Cost: $180–$200.*

Gold Creek Salmon Bake. This all-you-can-eat outdoor meal includes Alaska king salmon barbecued over an open alderwood fire. After dinner, you can walk in the woods, explore an abandoned mine, or pan for gold. *1½–2 hrs. Cost: $25.*

Ketchikan

This is one of the best places to sign on for a fishing charter. Ketchikan is also known for its authentic totem poles and nearby Misty Fjords National Monument, one of Alaska's best flightseeing adventures.

Adventure
Bicycle Tour. Ride along a gently rolling dirt road with spectacular views of the ocean and coastal mountains. Your guides will point out wildlife, talk about local history and geography, and take riders on a tour of a working fish hatchery. *3 hrs. Cost: $75.*

Flightseeing, Misty Fjords. Aerial views of granite cliffs that rise 4,000 ft from the sea, waterfalls, rain forests, and wildlife are topped off with a landing on a high wilderness lake. *2 hrs. Cost: $155–$180.*

Ketchikan by Kayak. Board an easy-to-paddle sea kayak for a whale's-eye view of the historic Ketchikan waterfront and nearby wilderness. *2–2½ hrs. Cost: $65–$85.*

Mountain Lake Canoe Adventure. You and your guide paddle across a mountain lake in oversize canoes (fast, stable, easy to maneuver) and watch for eagles roosting in the trees. *3½ hrs. Cost: $75–$85.*

Sportfishing. Cast your line for Alaska king and silver salmon or halibut along the Inside Passage. All equipment is provided, and you can buy your license on board. Group size is limited. Fish will be cleaned, and arrangements can be made to have your catch frozen or smoked and shipped home. *4–5 hrs. Cost: $140–$170.*

Cultural
Saxman Native Village. In a Native village displaying more than 20 totem poles and where the inhabitants still practice traditional arts, you'll learn much about the Tlingit culture. A visit here sometimes includes a tour of downtown Ketchikan. *2½ hrs. Cost: $45.*

Totem and Cannery Tour. You'll learn about Ketchikan's Native and pioneer history as you visit the Totem Heritage Center, which preserves some of Alaska's oldest totem poles, and the George Inlet Cannery, one of 14 that once lined Ketchikan's shores. *3½ hrs. Cost: $50.*

Petersburg

The fishing community of Petersburg, with its Scandinavian-style homes, still reflects the heritage of the Norwegians who settled here in the late nineteenth century.

Scenic
LeConte Flightseeing. One of the best flightseeing tours in Alaska takes you to the southernmost calving glacier in North America. *45-min flight. Cost: $128.*

Little Norway. Here's a chance to get outside of town and see the scenery. The tour also includes Norwegian refreshments and a performance of Norwegian dance at the Sons of Norway Hall. *2 hrs. Cost: $26.*

Walking Tour. A guide will relate the history and fishing heritage of Petersburg as you explore the old part of town on foot. *1½ hrs. Cost: $10.*

Seward

This tiny town, nestled against the mountains on Prince William Sound, is the port for Anchorage. There's not much to see in this one-horse town, but the surrounding wilderness, most of it federal land, is beautiful.

Scenic

Log Cabin/Best of Seward. An orientation tour shows you life in a small Alaskan town. Watch for wildlife while journeying through Resurrection River valley. You'll visit Exit Glacier and spend some time in a log-cabin home listening to the owners spin tales of their interesting lifestyle and petting their sled dogs. *4–4½ hrs. Cost: $85–$100.*

Portage Glacier. Passengers disembarking in Seward should take advantage of the chance to see Portage Glacier, one of Alaska's famous "drive-up" glaciers. Note that you do have to take a boat from the visitors center to see the glacial face, which has receded dramatically in recent years. The drive along Turnagain Arm to Portage Glacier is one of Alaska's most beautiful. *4½–5 hrs. Cost: $95.*

Seward, Exit Glacier, and Sled Dogs. This tour will take you on a journey along the Resurrection River valley to Exit Glacier, one of Alaska's famous "drive-up" glaciers, inside Kenai Fjords National Park. It's the only part of the park accessible by road. A stop at an Alaskan sled-dog training center follows. *2 hrs. Cost: $50.*

Sitka

Sitka was the capital of Russian Alaska. Good walkers can easily do the town on foot. Otherwise, consider taking the town tour so you don't miss the eagle hospital and the 15 totem poles and towering trees of Sitka National Historical Park. This is also a good port for fishing.

Adventure

Sitka by Sea Kayak. The unique setting of Sitka against the backdrop of the Mount Edgecumb volcano provides a scenic stage for exploring the coastline by water. *3 hrs. Cost: $90.*

Sportfishing. Try for the salmon and halibut that are abundant in these waters. All equipment is provided; you buy your license on board. Your catch can be frozen and shipped. *4 hrs. Cost: $140–$170.*

Cultural

History and Nature Tour. A guided walk through Sitka shows off its political and natural history. This tour includes all the major sites plus a visit to the Sitka National Historic Park for a stroll through the rain forest. *2½ hrs. Cost: $45.*

Sitka Drive. If you'd rather not walk the town, this guided tour includes stops at the Sheldon Jackson Museum, Castle Hill, Sitka National Historic Park, and St. Michael's Cathedral. Sometimes you can see a performance by the New Archangel Dancers, local women who have mastered the intricate timing and athletic feats required for this traditional style of dance. Some excursions include the fascinating Raptor Rehabilitation Center. *3 hrs. Cost: $30–$45.*

Nature

Eagle Hospital and City Tour. After a tour of historic Sitka, visit the Alaska Raptor Rehabilitation Center, where injured birds of prey are nursed back to health. *3 hrs. Cost: $40.*

Sea Otter Quest. This search for the sea otter and other Sitka wildlife is a cruise-passenger favorite. It's sold aboard virtually every ship stopping here. Creatures that you're likely to see include whales, eagles, puffins, and more. *3 hrs. Cost: $100.*

Skagway

The wooden sidewalks and false-front buildings of Skagway, once the gateway to the Klondike, stir up memories of Gold Rush fever. The White Pass & Yukon Railroad excursion gives cruise passengers a chance to get high into the mountains.

Adventure

Chilkoot Trail Hike. A moderate hike along the famous Chilkoot trail brings you back to the Days of '98. This was one of the most popular routes to the Klondike goldfields. *3½ hrs. Cost: $50.*

Klondike Bicycle Tour. A van takes you to the top of the Klondike Pass, and you ride 15 mi downhill, enjoying the spectacular views of White Pass and Alaska's scenery along the way. Stops are made to take photographs of the area's glaciers, coastal mountains, and waterfalls. *2 hrs. Cost: $70.*

Cultural/Scenic

Skagway Streetcar. This trip is especially exciting for antique-car buffs, who can ride in the Skagway Streetcar Company's vintage 1930s cars. The tour through town to the Gold Rush Cemetery and Reid Falls is accompanied by a historical narrative. *2 hrs. Cost: $35–$40.*

White Pass & Yukon Railroad. The 20-mi trip in vintage railroad cars, on narrow-gauge tracks built to serve the Yukon goldfields, runs past the famous White Pass, skims along the edge of granite cliffs, crosses a 215-ft-high steel cantilever bridge over Dead Horse Gulch, climbs to 2,865 ft at White Pass Summit, and zigzags through dramatic scenery—including the actual Trail of '98, worn into the mountainside a century ago. It's a must for railroad buffs and great for children. *3½ hrs. Cost: $80–$90.*

Valdez

Valdez is the terminus for the 800-mi trans-Alaska pipeline. Surrounded by alpine scenery and spectacular waterfalls, Valdez has been called the "Switzerland of Alaska." The town can be walked, but there's not a whole lot to see. This is another good port for flightseeing.

Adventure

Columbia Glacier Floatplane Sightseeing. Enjoy aerial views of Valdez and of Shoup Glacier, as well as a section of the pipeline and its terminus. The highlight is touching down in the water for a close-up view of the massive Columbia Glacier. *1 hr. Cost: $140–$180.*

Keystone River Rafting. This 1½-hour raft trip goes down the Lowe River, through a scenic canyon, and past the spectacular Bridal Veil Falls, which cascade 900 ft down the canyon wall. The bus trip from the ship is narrated. *2 hrs. Cost: $60–$70.*

Valdez by Sea Kayak. Bald eagles, sea birds, and seals are among the local residents you may encounter during this soft-adventure tour of the waters surrounding Valdez. *2½ hrs. Cost: $65.*

Cultural

Pipeline Story. With this tour you can visit the pipeline terminus and hear tales of how the pipeline was built. This is the only way to get into this high-security area. *2½ hrs. Cost: $20–$30.*

Vancouver, British Columbia

Unless you're on a longer cruise that begins in Los Angeles or San Francisco, Vancouver will likely be your first or last stop. If you're sailing round-trip, you'll get on and off the ship in Vancouver. Because most passengers are busy transferring between the airport and the ship, few shore excursions are scheduled. If you plan to stay in Vancouver before or after your cruise, most lines sell pre- or post-cruise city packages.

For cruise passengers on longer cruises, a call in Vancouver will be much like any other port call: you'll disembark just for the day and have the option of taking a ship-organized tour or exploring independently.

Cultural

City Tour. If this is your first visit to Vancouver, you may want to consider a city tour, a convenient way to see all the sights of this cosmopolitan city—the largest you'll visit on an Alaska cruise. Highlights include the Gastown district, Chinatown, and Stanley Park. *3 hrs. Cost: $29.*

Vancouver Pre- or Post-Cruise Package. Cruise-line land packages are an easy way to extend your cruise vacation without making separate arrangements. Usually, you'll have a choice of one, two, or three nights in town. Often, you'll also have a choice of hotels in different price ranges. Most packages include sightseeing tours and transfers between the ship and the hotel. Meals are generally extra unless noted in the brochure; transfers between the airport and hotel may be included only for air-sea passengers. Check with your cruise line or travel agent for the exact terms of your Vancouver package.

Victoria, British Columbia

Victoria is best known for its British traditions and gardens, which are the focal point of the most popular shore excursions.

Cultural/Scenic
Grand City Drive and Afternoon High Tea. This is a good choice for Anglophiles and others with an interest in Victoria's British heritage. The drive through downtown, past Craigdarroch Castle and residential areas, finishes with a British-style high tea at a hotel. A variation of this excursion takes visitors on a tour of the castle in lieu of high tea. *3½ hrs. Cost: $35.*

Short City Tour and Butchart Gardens. Drive through key places of interest, such as the city center and residential areas, on the way to Butchart Gardens—a must for garden aficionados. *3½ hrs. Cost: $39.*

Wrangell

This small island community is one of the oldest towns in Alaska and the only one to have been governed under three flags—imperial Russian, British, and American. Its most unusual attractions are the petroglyphs—prehistoric boulder carvings found on a nearby beach.

Cultural
City Tour. Explore Native history at Shakes Island, the Wrangell Museum, and Petroglyph Beach. *2 hrs. Cost: $20.*

Sawmill. Get a behind-the-scenes view of Alaska's largest and most modern sawmill. *Cost: $30.*

4 The Alaska Cruise Fleet

The Alaska cruise fleet is diverse: passenger capacities range from nearly 2,000 people to only a dozen. Lifestyle aboard these ships also spans the range, from elegant to a more rugged expedition-style atmosphere, depending on the type of ship and its onboard facilities. Bigger ships tend to be more formal, especially when it comes to evening dress. Smaller ships are more casual, and the dress code for dinner is usually "come as you are." For more information on different types of ships, *see* Chapter 1.

Ocean Liners

Crystal Harmony. The *Crystal Harmony* is exceptionally sleek and sophisticated. Spacious and well equipped, the ship has plenty of open deck space for watching the scenery plus a forward observation lounge with oversize windows, set high above the bridge. Overall, this is one of Alaska's most spacious and elegant vessels. Cabins are especially roomy; more than half have a private veranda. *Crystal Cruises, 2121 Avenue of the Stars, Los Angeles, CA 90067, tel. 310/785–9300 or 800/446–6620. Built: 1990. Size: 49,400 tons. Capacity: 940 passengers. Norwegian and Japanese officers and an international crew. 7 bars, 6 entertainment lounges, fitness center with massage and sauna, casino, cinema, library, video arcade, smoking room. Cabin amenities: 24-hr room service, refrigerator, robes, TV-VCR. Average per diem: $400–$500.*

Galaxy and ***Mercury.*** With features like video walls and interactive television systems in cabins, both ships are high-tech pioneers, yet at the same time are elegant, warm, and well-appointed. For example, the ships' spas are some of the best at sea. Large windows (including a dramatic two-story wall of glass in the dining room and wraparound windows in the Stratosphere Lounge, the gym, and beauty salon) and glass sunroofs over the pools bathe the ships in natural light and afford excellent views of Alaska's natural beauty. *Celebrity Cruises, 5200 Blue Lagoon Dr., Miami, FL 33126, tel. 800/437–3111. Built: 1996/1997. Size: 77,713 tons. Capacity: 1,870 passengers. Greek officers and an international crew. 11 bar-lounges; golf simulator; health club with massage, sauna, and thalassotherapy pool; casino; video-game room; library; playroom. Cabin amenities: 24-*

hr room service, butler service in suites, minibar, TV. Average per diem: $400–$500.

Jubilee. The *Jubilee* brings Carnival's "Fun Ship" style of cruising to the Last Frontier. The ship offers plenty of open space and has many resortlike qualities, though the Jubilee is not nearly as sharp and state-of-the-art as Carnival's newer vessels. The interior decor is modern and festive, incorporating the entire spectrum of colors. Cabins are of similar size and appearance throughout the ship, comfortable and larger than average; the majority have twin beds that can be made into a king-size bed. Most outside cabins have large square windows rather than portholes. *Carnival Cruise Lines, Carnival Pl., 3655 N.W. 87th Ave., Miami, FL 33178, tel. 800/327–9501. Built: 1986. Size: 47,262 tons. Capacity: 1,486 passengers. Italian officers and an international crew. 7 bars, 6 entertainment lounges, fitness center with massage and sauna, casino, video-game room, library, playroom. Cabin amenities: 24-hr room service, TV. Average per diem: $200–$300.*

Nieuw Amsterdam. More traditionally styled than the newest and snazziest ships, the *Nieuw Amsterdam*'s highlight is its multimillion-dollar collection of 17th- and 18th-century antiques. Outside deck areas are rather small, but the wraparound promenade is ideally suited for taking in the passing view. The Crow's Nest observation lounge is an especially elegant and atmospheric perch for a rainy day on the Inside Passage. Compared with most newer ships, other facilities are on the modest size, especially the gym and the single-level dining room. Outside staterooms are spacious, however. Tipping is optional, but passengers tend to tip anyway. A naturalist and a Native artist in residence sail aboard each Alaska cruise, and the Passport to Fitness Program encourages a healthy diet and exercise. *Holland America Line Westours, 300 Elliott Ave. W, Seattle, WA 98119, tel. 206/281–3535 or 800/426–0327. Built: 1983. Size: 33,930 tons. Capacity: 1,214 passengers. Dutch officers and Indonesian and Filipino crew. 7 bars, 3 entertainment lounges, fitness center with massage and sauna, casino, cinema, video-game room, library. Cabin amenities: 24-hr room service, TV. Average per diem: $400–$500.*

Norwegian Sky. The *Norwegian Sky* will be Alaska's newest cruise ship when it makes its Alaska debut in May 2000, and it comes with all the bells and whistles of Alaska's biggest ships, from alternative dining options to an Internet Café. But what's most significant about the Sky is its homeport—Seattle. It's the only big cruise ship to sail in and out of this American city rather than Vancouver, which eliminates the three-hour drive between the airport and the city (most cruise passengers fly into Seattle and transfer to Vancouver by motorcoach or vice-versa). *Norwegian Cruise Line, 7665 Corporate Center Dr., Miami, FL 33126, tel. 305/436–0866 or 800/327–7030. Built: 1999. Size: 80,000 tons. Capacity: 2,002 passengers. Norwegian officers and an international crew. 12 bars and entertainment lounges, fitness center with massage and sauna, casino, library, youth and teen centers. Cabin amenities: 24-hr room service, TV. Average per diem: $300–$400.*

Norwegian Wind. It's not the biggest or most extravagant ship afloat, but the *Norwegian Wind* is innovative and intelligently conceived. The most distinctive design features are its extensive terracing and abundant use of picture windows. Instead of one big dining room, three smaller restaurants create a more intimate ambience. Even the biggest, the Terraces, seats only 282 passengers on several levels and has windows on three sides for sea views; the Sun Terrace is similarly attractive. (You or your travel agent should specifically request an assignment in one of these two dining rooms.) The third dining room, the Four Seasons, is pretty but lacks the terraced layout and picture windows of the other rooms. Extensive use of floor-to-ceiling windows, terraced decks, a wraparound promenade, and picture windows in the cabins make this an ideal ship for taking in the passing scenery. Convertible sofas in the cabins, connecting staterooms, the activity-filled Kids Crew program, a playroom, and a video arcade with games, a jukebox, and a 45-inch color TV make this a good choice for family cruising. *Norwegian Cruise Line, 7665 Corporate Center Dr., Miami, FL 33126, tel. 305/435–0866 or 800/327–7030. Built: 1993. Size: 50,760 tons. Capacity: 1,748 passengers. Norwegian officers and an international crew. 13 bars and lounges, fitness center with massage and sauna, basketball court, casino, theater, library, youth center.*

Cabin amenities: 24-hr room service, TV. Average per diem: $300–$400.

Ocean Princess, Sea Princess, Dawn Princess, and **Sun Princess.** The brand-new *Ocean Princess,* and her sisters, *Sea Princess, Dawn Princess,* and *Sun Princess,* offer the greatest number of private balconies—more than 70% of outside cabins have them—of any ships sailing in Alaska. Each ship has two main showrooms and two main passenger dining rooms; an international food court with a 270-degree view over the bow of the ship; a pizzeria; a wine and caviar bar; and a patisserie for coffee and drinks. *Princess Cruises, 10100 Santa Monica Blvd., Los Angeles, CA 90067, tel. 310/553–1770 or 800/568–3262. Built: 2000/ 1995/1997/1998/. Size: 77,000 tons. Capacity: 1,950 passengers. Italian and British officers and European, American, and Filipino crew. 7 bars, 2 entertainment lounges, fitness center with massage and sauna, basketball court, golf simulator, casino, library, teen and children's center. Cabin amenities: 24-hr room service, refrigerator, robes, TV. Average per diem: $500–$600.*

Regal Princess. This futuristic white ship is unmistakable because of the white dome that tops the bridge. Underneath is a 13,000-square-ft entertainment and observation area with 270-degree views—perfect for a rainy day in Glacier Bay. A small observation deck below the bridge gives great views, and you're likely to have it all to yourself: it's so well-hidden, it's not even on the deck plan. There's a ⅛-mi high-traction outdoor running track, and the ship carries an impressive contemporary art collection. Cabins are quite spacious, and suites, minisuites, and some standard cabins have private verandas. *Princess Cruises, 10100 Santa Monica Blvd., Los Angeles, CA 90067, tel. 310/553–1770 or 800/568–3262. Built: 1991. Size: 70,000 tons. Capacity: 1,590 passengers. Italian officers and an international crew. 9 bars, 5 entertainment lounges, fitness center with massage and sauna, casino, cinema, library. Cabin amenities: 24-hr room service, refrigerator, robes, TV. Average per diem: $400–$500.*

Ryndam, Statendam, Volendam, and **Veedam.** These ships can best be described as classic-revival, combining the old and new in one neat package. From the outside they look bigger than they really are, thanks to their modern profile. Inside, they dramatically express Holland America's past in a two-tier dining room, replete with dual grand staircases framing an orchestra balcony—the latter first introduced on the *Nieuw Amsterdam* of 1938. Although the ships are structurally identical, Holland America has given each its own distinct personality in the layout and decor of the public rooms. An abundance of glass, outdoor deck space, and a retractable roof over the main pool make these good ships for Alaska cruising. Great views can be found along the wraparound promenade, from the top-deck observation lounge, and in the glass-lined dining room. All standard outside cabins come with a small sitting area and a real tub; some have private verandas. Tipping is optional, but passengers tend to tip anyway. A naturalist and a Native artist in residence sail aboard each Alaska cruise, and the Passport to Fitness Program encourages a healthy diet and exercise. *Holland America Line Westours, 300 Elliott Ave. W, Seattle, WA 98119, tel. 206/ 281–3535 or 800/426–0327. Built: 1994/1993/1999/1993. Size: 55,451 tons (Volendam 63,000 tons). Capacity: 1,266 passengers (Volendam 1,440). Dutch officers and Indonesian and Filipino crew. 7 bars and lounges, fitness center with massage and sauna, casino, cinema. Cabin amenities: 24-hr room service, TV. Average per diem: $400–$500.*

Sky Princess. This ship combines an old-liner atmosphere with the modern touches passengers expect from a cruise ship. The showroom is one of the biggest afloat, and public spaces are appointed with a notable collection of contemporary art. Most public rooms command good views of the sea. The Horizon Lounge, for example, has floor-to-ceiling windows and a view directly over the bow—perfect for sailing in scenic waters. The two dining rooms are of intimate size, are identical in decor, and have windows that provide a reasonably good view of the passing scene. Cabins are spacious. Suites have verandas and bathtubs. *Princess Cruises, 10100 Santa Monica Blvd., Los Angeles, CA 90067, tel. 310/553–1770 or 800/568–3262. Built: 1984. Size: 46,314 tons. Capacity: 1,200 passengers. British officers and European international crew. 7 bars, 4 entertainment lounges, fitness center with massage and sauna, library, youth and teen centers. Cabin amenities: 24-hr room service, robes, TV. Average per diem: $400–$500.*

Universe Explorer. World Explorer Cruises' strong suit is education, and passengers should not expect the glitz and glamour of some newer ships. The line's vessel (formerly the *Enchanted Seas* of Commodore Cruise Line) was built as a transatlantic liner, but World Explorer has modified it to serve as a floating classroom. Rather than the disco and casino typically found on cruise ships, the *Universe Explorer* has an herbarium and a 15,000-volume library—the largest at sea. Several other public rooms include a forward observation lounge. The *Universe Explorer*'s itinerary incorporates long port stays and an excellent array of shore excursions. On any given sailing, you may travel in the company of four or five experts in history, art, geology, marine life, music, or geography. Cabins are simple and spacious. *World Explorer Cruises, 555 Montgomery St., San Francisco, CA 94111, tel. 415/393–1565 or 800/854–3835. Built: 1958. Size: 23,500 tons. Capacity: 739 passengers. International officers and crew. 4 bars, 5 lounges, fitness center with massage, cinema, card room, library, youth center. Cabin amenities: Color TV. Average per diem: $200–$300.*

Vision of the Seas and **Rhapsody of the Seas.** The *Vision* and the *Rhapsody* have dramatic balconied dining rooms and tiered showrooms. For great views of the passing scenery, each ship has a "Viking Crown Lounge" on the uppermost deck with wraparound glass. The indoor/outdoor deck areas of the Solarium Spas are especially well suited to cruising in often rainy Alaska. The *Rhapsody* and *Vision* have relatively large cabins and more balconies than Royal Caribbean's previous megaships. About one fourth of the cabins have private verandas. The ships also have specially designed family suites with separate bedrooms for parents and children. *Royal Caribbean Cruise Line, 1050 Caribbean Way, Miami, FL 33132, tel. 800/327–6700 (reservations); 800/255–4373 (brochures). Built: 1997/ 1998. Size: 78,491 tons. Capacity: 2,000 passengers. Norwegian officers and an international crew. 8 bars, 3 lounges, fitness center with massage and sauna, casino, theater, library, youth center. Cabin amenities: 24-hr room service, TV. Average per diem: $300–$400.*

Westerdam. As with other Holland America ships, the *Westerdam* carries a multimillion- dollar art collection that evokes the cruise line's storied history. Perhaps most impressive is an antique bronze cannon, cast in Rotterdam, which is strategically positioned in the center of the ship. Also worthy of note is the dining room. Unlike many newer ships with restaurants occupying a strategic perch with expansive views, the *Westerdam*'s dining room is below decks. But Holland America has turned a negative into a positive; the room is attractively accented with wood, brass, and traditional portholes. Cabins are large, with plenty of storage space; all but the least expensive have a sitting area with a convertible couch. Tipping is optional, but passengers tend to tip anyway. A resident naturalist sails aboard each Alaska cruise, and the Passport to Fitness Program encourages exercise and a healthy diet. *Holland America Line Westours, 300 Elliott Ave. W, Seattle, WA 98119, tel. 206/281–3535 or 800/426–0327. Built: 1986. Size: 53,872 tons. Capacity: 1,494 passengers. Dutch officers and Indonesian and Filipino crew. 7 bars, 2 entertainment lounges, fitness center with massage and sauna, casino, cinema, library, videogame room. Cabin amenities: 24-hr room service, TV. Average per diem: $400–$500.*

Small Ships

Expedition Ship

World Discoverer. This true expedition vessel, with a shallow draft and ice-hardened hull, is well equipped for Zodiac landings in intriguing ports of call. Naturalists and other guest lecturers enhance the shoreside experience and give enrichment talks in the theater. Cabins are small, but all are outside. Fares include all shore excursions except flightseeing. *Society Expeditions, 2001 Western Ave., Suite 300, Seattle, WA 98121, tel. 800/548–8669. Built: 1974. Size: 3,724 tons. Capacity: 138 passengers. German and Filipino officers, European and Filipino crew, international cruise and lecturer staff. 2 bars, 2 lounges, small gym and sauna, observation lounge, cinema–lecture hall, library. Average per diem: $400–$500.*

Coastal Cruisers

Executive Explorer. As the name suggests, the *Executive Explorer* is a plush ship. Its appointments include rich wood paneling throughout; deep, padded armchairs in the main lounge; and a gallerylike display of nearly 100 Alaskan prints. The main lounge has forward-facing observation windows; the dining room has color TV monitors. Even the stairwells have picture windows for views of the passing scenery. Outside observation areas include a partially covered sundeck, which gives a lofty perspective four decks above the water—an unusually high perch for such a small ship. Cabins have more artwork, two more big picture windows (unusually large for a ship this size), roomy closets, and other cabin amenities not often found in small-ship cabins. *Glacier Bay Tours and Cruises, 520 Pike St., Suite 1400, Seattle, WA 98101, tel. 206/ 623–7110 or 800/451–5952 (U.S. and Canada). Built: 1986. Size: 98 tons. Capacity: 49 passengers. American officers and crew. Observation lounge. Cabin amenities: Minibar, refrigerator, color TV, VCR. Average per diem: $400–$500.*

Safari Spirit and **Safari Quest.** Alaska's smallest cruise ships are tiny even by small-ship standards, carrying just 22 and 12 passengers, respectively. Yet they come with all kinds of creature comforts usually associated with bigger ships, like all-suite accommodations—some with real tubs and queen-size beds. Both yachts have an "under the stars" outdoor hot tub. All drinks are included in the fare, including beer and wine, as are all shore excursions. A naturalist provides informal lectures and accompanies passengers on kayaking and fishing expeditions. *American Safari Cruises, 19101 36th Ave. W, Suite 201, Linnwood, WA 98036, tel. 425/776–8889 or 888/862–8881. Built: 1981/1992. Size: NA/97 tons. Capacity: 22/12 passengers. American officers and crew. Bar/lounge, solarium/library (Safari Quest only). Average per diem: $500–$600.*

Sea Bird and **Sea Lion.** These small, shallow-draft ships have the freedom to sail through narrow straits and visit out-of-the-way areas that are inaccessible to big ships. The boats forgo port calls at larger, busier towns and instead spend time making Zodiac raft landings, conducting wildlife searches, and stopping for beachcombing and barbecuing in Tracy Arm. These ships are not for claustrophobics, as the ship's storage capacity, the size of the crew, and the number of public areas have been cut back to carry 70 passengers. All cabins are technically outside staterooms, but

Category 1 rooms have only a high port light (a very small porthole). *Special Expeditions, 720 5th Ave., New York, NY 10019, tel. 212/765–7740 or 800/762–0003. Built: 1982/1981. Size: 100 tons. Capacity: 70 passengers. American officers and crew. Bar-lounge, library. Average per diem: $500–$600.*

Spirit of Alaska. Alaska Sightseeing's original overnight vessel is still its coziest. You are never by yourself in the lounge, and meals in the homey dining room resemble a family affair soon after the cruise has begun. Sleek and small, the *Spirit of Alaska* feels like a real yacht. A bow ramp adds to the sense of adventure, allowing passengers to put ashore at tiny islands and beaches few other cruise travelers visit. Toilets and showers are combined units. Suites and some outside cabins have TVs, but only for watching videos. *Alaska Sightseeing/Cruise West, 4th & Battery Bldg., Suite 700, Seattle, WA 98121, tel. 206/441–8687 or 800/426–7702. Built: 1980; refurbished: 1991. Size: 97 tons. Capacity: 82 passengers. American/Canadian officers and crew. Bar-lounge, exercise equipment. Average per diem: $400–$500.*

Spirit of Columbia. Although cut from the same mold as Alaska Sightseeing's *Spirit of Alaska,* this ship has one notable feature: a unique bow ramp design that allows passengers to walk directly on shore from the forward lounge. The interior design was inspired by the national-park lodges of the American West, with a color scheme based on muted shades of evergreen, rust, and sand. All suites and deluxe cabins have a mini-refrigerator, an armchair, and a small desk. The Owner's Suite stretches the width of the vessel; located just under the bridge, its row of forward-facing windows gives a captain's-eye view of the ship's progress. Suites and deluxe cabins have TVs, but only for watching videos. *Alaska Sightseeing/Cruise West, 4th & Battery Bldg., Suite 700, Seattle, WA 98121, tel. 206/441–8687 or 800/426–7702. Built: 1979; refurbished: 1994. Size: 98 tons. Capacity: 81 passengers. American/Canadian officers and crew. Bar-lounge, exercise equipment. Average per diem: $400–$500.*

Spirit of Discovery. Floor-to-ceiling windows in the main lounge provide stunning views of passing scenery for passengers aboard this snazzy cruiser. Blue-suede chairs, a wraparound bench sofa at the bow, and a mirrored ceiling make the chrome-filled lounge look especially swank. From here, passengers have direct access to a large outdoor viewing deck, one of two aboard. This is great for those who don't want to trudge upstairs every time a whale is spotted. Deluxe cabins have mini-refrigerators, and many cabins have extra-large picture windows; two cabins are reserved for single travelers. Toilets and showers are combined units. Suites and some outside cabins have TVs, but only for watching videos. *Alaska Sightseeing/Cruise West, 4th & Battery Bldg., Suite 700, Seattle, WA 98121, tel. 206/441–8687 or 800/426–7702. Built: 1976. Size: 94 tons. Capacity: 84 passengers. American/Canadian officers and crew. Bar-lounge, exercise equipment. Cabin amenities: Refrigerator and TV-VCR in deluxe cabins. Average per diem: $400–$500.*

Spirit of Endeavour. Alaska Sightseeing's newest flagship is also the line's largest. Oak and teak are used throughout the light and airy ship. All cabins are outside with large picture windows for superb views. Some cabins have connecting doors, which make them convenient for families traveling together, and all cabins have TVs, but only for watching videos. *Alaska Sightseeing/Cruise West, 4th & Battery Bldg., Suite 700, Seattle, WA 98121, tel. 206/441–8687 or 800/426–7702. Built: 1984; refurbished: 1996. Size: 99 tons. Capacity: 107 passengers. American/Canadian officers and crew. Bar, lounge, library. Cabin amenities: TV-VCR in all cabins and refrigerator in some. Average per diem: $500–$600.*

Spirit of Glacier Bay. Alaska Sightseeing's smallest overnight cruiser is nearly identical to the line's *Spirit of Alaska*, and its public rooms are even cozier. Wraparound couches and small table-and-chair groupings in the lounge create a living-room feel. Cabins on the lowest deck have no window, just a high port light, but soft, cream-color fabrics help brighten up the ship's tiny accommodations. Toilets and showers are combined units. There are no TVs in the cabins. *Alaska Sightseeing/Cruise West, 4th & Battery Bldg., Suite 700, Seattle, WA 98121, tel. 206/441–8687 or 800/426–7702. Built: 1971. Size: 98 tons. Capacity: 52 passengers. American/Canadian officers and crew. Bar-lounge. Average per diem: $400–$500.*

Spirit of '98. With its rounded stern and wheelhouse, old-fashioned smokestack, and Victorian decor, the *Spirit of '98* evokes the feel of a turn-of-the-century steamer. Inside and out, mahogany adorns this elegant ship. Overstuffed chairs upholstered in crushed velvet complete the Gold Rush–era motif. For private moments, there are plenty of nooks and crannies aboard the ship, along with the cozy Soapy's Parlor at the stern, with a small bar and a few tables and chairs. All cabins are outside with picture windows, and all have TVs, but only for watching videos. *Alaska Sightseeing/Cruise West, 4th & Battery Bldg., Suite 700, Seattle, WA 98121, tel. 206/441–8687 or 800/426–7702. Built: 1984; refurbished: 1993. Size: 96 tons. Capacity: 101 passengers. American/Canadian officers and crew. 2 bar-lounges, exercise equipment. Average per diem: $400–$500.*

Wilderness Adventurer and Wilderness Discoverer. The *Wilderness Adventurer* and the *Wilderness Discoverer*, formerly the *Mayan Prince* and now the latest addition to the Glacier Bay fleet, evoke the casual comforts of home. The coffee's always on, and you'll never need a jacket and tie for dinner. Alaskan art enhances the otherwise simple surroundings, and there's just enough varnished wood to impart a nautical feel. A library of books and videos has a nice selection of Alaska titles. There are no TVs in the cabins, but you can watch tapes—or your own wildlife footage—on the community VCR in the main lounge. The ships' greatest assets are the naturalists, who put their hearts into their work. They lead kayak excursions and shore walks and get as much of a thrill as the passengers do whenever wildlife is sighted. Cabins, like the rest of the ship, are simple and functional. Toilets and showers are combined units. Note that the *Wilderness Discoverer* does not have the sea kayaks that are the trademark of the *Wilderness Adventurer*. *Glacier Bay Tours and Cruises, 520 Pike St., Suite 1400, Seattle, WA 98101, tel. 206/623–7110 or 800/451–5952 (U.S. and Canada). Built: 1983/1992. Size: 89/98 tons. Capacity: 74 passengers (86 for the Discoverer). American officers and crew. Observation lounge. Average per diem: $400–$500.*

Wilderness Explorer. The *Wilderness Explorer* is billed as a "floating base camp" for "active adventure," and that's no exaggeration. Sea-kayak outings may last more than three hours (a 5-mi paddle). Discovery hikes cross dense thickets and climb rocky creek beds. You'll spend most of your time off the ship—which is a good thing, since you wouldn't want to spend much time on it. Decor-wise, the ship is pleasing enough—mostly late 1960s mod with a dash of Old World leather and even Greek Revival accents. But the public spaces are very limited and the cabins are positively tiny. This ship is not for the typical cruise passenger; it should be considered only by the serious outdoor enthusiast. *Glacier Bay Tours and Cruises, 520 Pike St., Suite 1400, Seattle, WA 98101, tel. 206/623–7110 or 800/451–5952 (U.S. and Canada). Built: 1969. Size: 98 tons. Capacity: 36 passengers. American officers and crew. Observation lounge. Average per diem: $300–$400.*

Yorktown Clipper. The *Yorktown Clipper* is a stylish coastal cruiser with a casual sophistication. There are only a few public rooms—which are bright and comfortable—and deck space is limited. On-board naturalists and Zodiac landing craft enhance the emphasis on destination. Floor-to-ceiling windows in the lounge and large windows in the dining room allow sightseeing in all weather. Cabins are all outside, and most have large windows. The crew is young and enthusiastic. *Clipper Cruise Lines, 7711 Bonhomme Ave., St. Louis, MO 63105, tel. 314/727–2929 or 800/325–0010. Built: 1988. Size: 97 tons. Capacity: 138 passengers. American officers and crew. Bar-lounge. Average per diem: $300–$400.*

Ferries

Alaska Marine Highway System. Travel by ferry is very scenic. It's also rather slow: maximum speed is 16.5 knots, compared with 21 knots or better for the typical ocean liner. But it's a great way to take in the landscape, collect your thoughts, jot down some notes in a journal—and maybe see a whale or two. The ferry also affords freedom of movement. Unlike the big cruise ships, which require passengers to follow a set itinerary, ferries come and go daily. So you can get on and off whenever you wish, and stay as long as you want. The shortest trip on the Alaska Marine Highway lasts only one hour; the longest route takes 37 hours to complete. You can book cabins for longer trips. A complete ferry itinerary can be planned in advance, or you can make it up as you go along, buying each ticket at the terminal on the day of your departure. However, reservations are strongly recommended in summer. Between ports of call, travelers get to see places that few other tourists visit. Stops are often made at smaller communities, like Angoon and Tenakee Springs—just a strip of houses on stilts huddled along the shoreline. Another advantage of ferry travel is cost: fares are affordable, and the cafeteria-style food is hearty and cheap. While the ferries are less than luxurious, they certainly are comfortable enough. Each has a glass-lined observation lounge, and the larger ferries have a bar. Cabins on the Alaskan ferries are simple but serviceable. They book up almost instantly for cruises during the summer season, but a number of tour operators sell packages that include accommodations. One of the oldest and largest is Knightly Tours (Box 16366, Seattle, WA 98116, tel. 206/938–8567 or 800/426–2123). *Alaska Marine Highway System, Box 25535, Juneau, AK 99802, tel. 800/642–0066.*

INDEX

NOTES

NOTES

NOTES